PARTNER
for
PERFORMANCE

Strategically Aligning Learning and Development

Ingrid Guerra-López
and Karen Hicks

© 2017 ASTD DBA the Association for Talent Development (ATD)
All rights reserved. Printed in the United States of America.

20 19 18 17   1 2 3 4 5

No part of this publication may be reproduced, distributed, or transmitted in any form or by any means, including photocopying, recording, or other electronic or mechanical methods, without the prior written permission of the publisher, except in the case of brief quotations embodied in critical reviews and certain other noncommercial uses permitted by copyright law. For permission requests, please go to www.copyright.com, or contact Copyright Clearance Center (CCC), 222 Rosewood Drive, Danvers, MA 01923 (telephone: 978.750.8400; fax: 978.646.8600).

ATD Press is an internationally renowned source of insightful and practical information on talent development, workplace learning, and professional development.

ATD Press
1640 King Street
Alexandria, VA 22314 USA

Ordering information: Books published by ATD Press can be purchased by visiting ATD's website at www.td.org/books or by calling 800.628.2783 or 703.683.8100.

Library of Congress Control Number: 2017941607

ISBN-10: 1-56286-581-1
ISBN-13: 978-1-56286-581-8
e-ISBN: 978-1-56286-582-5

ATD Press Editorial Staff
Director: Kristine Luecker
Manager: Melissa Jones
Community of Practice Manager, Senior Leaders & Executives: Ann Parker
Developmental Editor: Jack Harlow
Editor: Christian Green
Text Design: Tony Julien
Cover Design: Jen Huppert, Jen Huppert Design
Printed by Versa Press Inc., East Peoria, IL

Contents

Introduction

There are a considerable number of sources on strategically aligning training to the business. Unfortunately, most of the literature about strategic alignment, particularly within learning and talent development, is fundamentally flawed. Much of what has already been written comes from a preimposed solution mindset and, in many cases, a training mindset. Loose associations between how much an organization spends on training and the organization's success are often touted; however, what is referred to as a "strategic alignment approach" typically consists of a solution-driven analysis and design process.

What's wrong with that, you might ask? This training mindset illustrates an inherent bias toward familiar solutions, rather than ensuring organizational accomplishments. While analysis and design may improve the look and feel of the solution, they often do little to improve the organization's strategic results. No amount of analysis and design will deliver worthwhile results if you have picked the wrong solution.

Our experience over the last few decades—along with feedback from clients, colleagues, and students, as well as support from the research literature—indicates that our ability to deliver meaningful results rests on genuinely and actively collaborating with our clients to address problems and opportunities. This has important implications for what we are expected to do and deliver.

Partner for Performance sets out to help you, the L&D professional, establish partnerships that measurably contribute to organizational success—and provide you with a practical set of frameworks, processes, tools, and skills to meet those expectations effectively. Helping or adding value requires a consultative approach in which you partner with clients—whether you work within an organization or offer your services as an external party—to collaboratively define, understand, and address important performance problems and opportunities. This consultative approach is based on trust, openness, and authenticity. If a client submits a request you think won't help, and perhaps even make matters worse, you must be able to say so compellingly and empathetically.

A consultative approach requires you to ask questions—a lot of questions—that come from a "help me understand" mindset, rather than to assume you always have the perfect solution in mind. Given that clients know their context better than you ever will, opening the relationship with a line of questioning allows you to help them recognize the underlying, interrelated symptoms behind a problem.

Recognizing the integrated nature of organizations—creating fit among organizational activities in relation to internal and external environments—is a critical aspect of strategic alignment. Strategically oriented organizations do not want to waste time, energy, or money on activities that aren't essential to success. They connect action to a value-added purpose that interacts with and reinforces other activities. They carefully consider how to deploy their resources to the processes that will have the greatest impact on their strategic priorities.

L&D professionals will succeed and thrive if they view their roles as much more than mere deliverers of learning services and products, and instead form partnerships with managers to drive performance aligned to the strategic priorities by generating, sharing, and using timely and relevant performance data to support decision making and action.

To influence how L&D professionals view themselves and their role, this book will use the term *performance improvement professionals* interchangeably with L&D professionals. It is important to stay focused on performance and broaden your range of tools and approaches for improving it. Your sustained value depends on moving out of familiar frameworks, actions, processes, knowledge, and even job titles and roles to expand beyond your comfort zones.

The focus of the alignment process described in this book is to ensure a clear and measurable relationship between L&D initiatives and the strategic priorities of the organization. This book also introduces a framework for assessing, designing, and evaluating the alignment of learning and development as a functional unit by what they do and how they do it.

How This Book Is Organized

The first two chapters provide the conceptual framework for the approach to strategic alignment. While two foundation chapters might seem a bit long for some, we believe that before you commit to shifting your approach you must have a compelling rationale for doing so, as well as a clear idea of what strategic alignment is and is not. Chapter 1 describes the evolving realities and expanded context within which L&D professionals must make contributions. Chapter 2 provides a thorough discussion about how we approach alignment, and the key considerations L&D professionals face as they seek to support desirable change and consequences in their organizations.

Then you'll go through the detailed process for strategically aligning L&D solutions to organizational priorities. Chapter 3 covers the first major phase of strategic alignment: uncovering stakeholder perceptions and expectations. Chapter 4 details the process for gathering empirical evidence to strengthen how you define problems and opportunities. Chapter 5 describes how to analyze causal factors and use those factors to select innovative solutions. Chapter 6 introduces the key elements for designing effective workplace implementation and transfer strategies.

Finally, we present the framework for aligning the entire L&D functional unit of an organization to support strategic priorities through performance-driven mechanisms and processes. The appendix provides readers with a full list of tools used throughout this book for easy reference, replication, and customization.

The Real Value of L&D

Organizations are critical components of our social fiber. Whether government institutions or nongovernment organizations, business or nonprofit, healthcare, education, or military, they are a major engine of economic and social activity. We all have a stake in their effective functioning, and L&D professionals in particular can play a key role in their sustainable success.

Organizations have strategic goals they strive to achieve, as well as operational imperatives to help reach these strategic goals. They choose strategies that enable them to achieve a competitive advantage and remain sustainable. Members execute strategies to sustain, grow, or develop the organization's position within the marketplace. Organizations that reach their goals with greater efficiencies and effectiveness recognize the dynamic realities and the possibilities for aligning performance at every level of the organization.

Organizations that use performance-driven processes to improve the competence of their people have found a consistent way to ensure that the right people are communicating with one another about the right things, thus better aligning their programs and services with their needs and building stronger relationships with organizational leaders. This requires a paradigm shift in how L&D professionals view their role and how they align their work to organizational objectives and strategies through enhanced partnerships with management. These partnerships grow over time, and they begin by focusing on important shared needs and the belief that the partnership will be conducive to meeting those needs.

Smart organizations refer to their people as their competitive advantage, because they make the difference. Think about your interactions with companies. Would you pay a little more for a product if you knew you would receive exceptional service? Would you choose to purchase products or services from an organization whose quality was inconsistent or unreliable? As a customer, you consider such criteria to decide with which organizations you choose to do business.

One of the primary functions of L&D professionals is developing workforce capabilities to maximize the competitive advantage organizations receive from their employees. By focusing your efforts and solutions on leveraging and developing this advantage, you align L&D to business needs—and generate real value.

And yet, talent development solutions, while at the heart of organizational success, can be expensive endeavors for organizations. Organizations rightly question their value when not clearly linked to strategic priorities before their selection and design. To ensure sound decisions regarding talent development strategies, L&D professionals must identify the tangible results that are gained from performance improvement efforts. Doing so leads to solutions that measurably help the organization achieve strategic objectives, and provides L&D professionals with hard evidence of their contribution to organizational success. Documenting these successes is critical for the function's growth, credibility, and sustainability as a true strategic partner.

The value of L&D should not be measured by the size of its budget, how many initiatives it launched, or how many people participated in its programs. These measures simply indicate resources (money and time) consumed and hours worked. Rather, value comes from the quantifiable improvement in human and organizational performance.

A Paradigm Shift

Consider your last talent development initiative and reflect on whether you had clear answers to the following questions before it was selected and designed:

- What factors influence human performance in the workplace, and how do they relate to one another?
- Which factors will the initiative affect? What do you know and what do you assume you know? What evidence do you have that it will be effective?
- What human performance results do you expect after the initiative?
- How will you measure the initiative's impact on organizational performance?
- How will the organizational structure support or hinder the changes in human performance you expect to see?
- What changes to the work environment must occur to realize expected results?
- How will you maintain desired workplace performance?

We believe the most important paradigm shift a performance improvement professional can make is to move beyond a solution-driven mindset and instead adopt a performance-driven mindset. It goes beyond the obsolete approach of simply fulfilling a training request. The answers will clarify strategic priorities, the use of resources, and even how products and services are offered to clients.

What would your stakeholders consider to be a valuable use of learning and talent development initiatives? What returns and benefits has your organization received for the investment in learning and talent development? Organizations that can demonstrate strategic alignment and use performance data to inform their actions and justify resource spending have a much better chance at sustainable organizational contributions and success. In this book, we provide a process for demonstrating this alignment and generating the data required to make sound decisions about learning and talent development.

An Expanding Mindset

While your organization might only think of performance improvement efforts as expenses, you can change these perceptions with a new mindset to carrying out your work. To start, you need to think of organizations as a system and expand the role you play within that system.

Consider your own performance for a moment. Are your behaviors or how you approach your work specific to the context of your organization? How does the organizational culture influence your interactions with others, your work output, your accountability for results, or the expectations others have of you? How do the tools and resources available to you influence your performance? W. Edwards Deming, one of the leading management thinkers of our time argued that "a bad system will beat a good person every time." This describes the power of an organizational system and how critical it is for performance improvement professionals to think about their work and its influence on the performance within the system, as well as the performance of others in their organizations.

Interactions with the work environment influence performance. For successful implementation of your performance improvement initiatives, you must understand your organization's anatomy and how your work fits within this anatomy. The importance of developing your ability to synthesize issues and elements throughout the organization cannot be overstated. Analysis of the issues is important, but it is not sufficient. You must not only look at performance problems in detail, but you must also look for how those problems relate to the system structure, culture, and other key organizational elements.

Consider the analogy of human anatomy. The body consists of many parts working together, interacting as one human system. Your arm does not operate independently of your shoulder. When you feel pain, you visit the doctor who examines where it hurts and what triggers the pain. How does this pain affect other parts of your body? How do other parts of your body influence the pain? How would various treatment options affect not only what hurts, but also other parts of your body? How will taking two medications concurrently affect you? Just as the doctor considers the whole body, you must consider all parts of the organizational system when opportunities for improvement are needed. You can do this by reverse engineering performance in organizations—start with the goal in mind, uncover the important factors (and their relationship) for reaching the goal, and engineer human performance in alignment with organizational performance.

Strategic business partnerships are the new way to do business in L&D roles. It is an alliance you form, over time, with your stakeholders and decision makers to ensure the work you do is strategically valuable and produces desired results for the organization. These partnerships also facilitate your desire to take an active role in the decisions that affect human performance in organizations. If you want a seat at the table, you must proactively think, behave, and perform like a strategic partner.

Note that your initial involvement might be driven by your technical expertise, so your technical perspective and advice are critical. However, for your technical expertise to have maximum impact, you must also demonstrate business acumen and certain personal attributes that support a trusting relationship with your clients. For example, imagine yourself in a meeting with high-level management. They are concerned about the changing patterns in consumer behavior and how they are influencing sales revenue, yet the focus of your observations are on reducing cognitive load of sales trainees. Do you think that enhances your credibility as a strategic business partner?

Your expertise about how people learn and perform should be conveyed in a way that concretely resonates with your partners and builds trust in your ability to help drive worthy results.

The following examples highlight what the requestor is looking for when establishing a strategic partnership, and how you may engage or demonstrate this skill, behavior, or attribute. As you read these, you may want to consider adding additional items you consider important:

- **Business Acumen:**
  - You understand the emerging needs of the business.
  - You know the business value chain.
  - You communicate in business language (written and verbal).
  - You understand the context in which the business operates.
  - You are aware of what is necessary to execute the organization's strategies.
  - You understand how your efforts are linked to the organization's mission.
- **Personal Attributes:**
  - You use teamwork to approach problem solving and decision making.
  - You have good communication skills.
  - You are caring.
  - You work proactively and continuously to develop and foster trust.
  - You are sincere in your desire to create win-win outcomes for those who will influence and be influenced by the solution.

- You are responsive to business and personal needs and can balance them.
- You are transparent with your work.
- You work proactively to gain support from management.
- **Technical Skills:**
  - You provide the business case for all learning decisions.
  - You plan how to integrate learning solutions throughout the organization.
  - You conduct a needs assessment to inform the selection, design, and delivery of strategic solutions.
  - You offer just-in-time learning solutions to address current business needs.

Essential Skills for the New Generation of L&D Professionals

To support this reverse engineering approach to performance improvement, it is critically important to be aware of the cognitive habits that drive your technical tasks and behaviors as you seek to improve human and organizational performance. These cognitive skills frame your view of the world and, in turn, how you approach your technical work. This provides a strong, flexible, and scalable base for understanding performance problems in their unique contexts, and selecting the best solution across a variety of situations.

If the L&D function is going to evolve to provide real value to the organization, it must take a system view of the organization to understand the relationships and interactions across various issues, events, and consequences. It must also apply strategic thinking to clarify where the organization wants to go, where it currently is in relation to that destination, and how to best get there. Critical thinking is foundational for both system and strategic thinking; those who don't master basic critical thinking skills are not likely to go far within the organization. Likewise, collaboration skills are key to getting things done. Organizations comprise groups of people who must partner effectively to make things happen and achieve results.

System thinking, strategic thinking, and critical thinking are all complementary processes that the new generation of L&D professionals will have to master to build credibility, become strategic partners to management, and add real value to the organization. These skills are not necessarily new, but they must be further developed and consistently applied from a broader perspective.

Next, let's delve into the specific tasks and steps associated with each of these core skills. It should be noted that while design thinking is not discussed specifically, these core skills are also the foundation for design thinking. These core skills will later be linked to the strategic alignment process.

System Thinking

Systems thinking is a management discipline that is concerned with the understanding of a system by examining the linkages and interactions between the components that comprise the whole system. In this book, we use the term *system* instead of *systems* as a reminder that strategic alignment requires we deal with the whole system, not just the subsystems (Kaufman 2000). The system thinking approach to problem solving and decision making identifies the impact of a problem (and potential solutions) on various segments of the organization (personnel, departments, customers, suppliers, and so forth). It is a way of thinking about how people, processes, and structures work together in organizations to see the patterns and cycles of performance in your organization. Rather than perceiving performance issues as isolated, you can see the relationships and interactions among various parts of the organization. This view is holistic and essential to gaining an understanding and appreciation for how any performance solution will perform within the organization. For performance improvement practitioners, this means approaching requests for solutions as triggers for diagnosis and alignment. System thinking helps you focus on the root causes of performance problems and their interrelated nature, and highlights which initiatives are likely to successfully address those root causes—and which are not likely to help, and perhaps even aggravate the situation in the long run.

Strategic Thinking

Strategic thinking is a long-term perspective to problem solving and decision making where performance improvement practitioners think from multiple timeframes with a focus on what has to be accomplished to achieve desired results. A strategic thinking approach to performance improvement offers opportunities to generate value, specifically aimed at the strategic priorities of organizations. You can purposefully facilitate this strategic value by creating the links, or fit, between the work you do and the value it ultimately adds to your organization. Strategic thinking involves adhering to objective analysis; planning ahead; thinking of how people, processes, and structures fit together; focusing on the organization's unique advantage or differentiator; and identifying gaps between where the organization is today and where it wants to be in the future and devising appropriately aligned improvements to help the organization realize desired results

Critical Thinking

Performance improvement practitioners apply critical thinking to analyze, synthesize, and evaluate information that supports decision making. These critical thinking activities are carried throughout the strategic alignment process. Some examples are:

- developing an orderly approach to prioritize tasks based on severity and urgency
- applying metacognitive knowledge that allows them to monitor their own performance
- determining credibility of sources and synthesizing this information to formulate and communicate decisions
- generating an objective, reasoned method to select among several solution options
- presenting a coherent and persuasive argument for decisions to different audiences.

Collaboration

Performance improvement work in organizations is highly collaborative. You work with others to problem solve, make decisions, implement those decisions, and evaluate the results of those decisions. You work toward common goals with the intent of achieving positive results for those within, and outside, the organization. A collaborative approach to performance improvement is central to changing the expectations and perceived value of your work. It involves representation for all stakeholders and gives explicit attention to cross-functional dialogue. Such relationship building creates a joint effort to helping your stakeholders and organizations reach their goals, and ultimately, to improve the perceptions and utility of your efforts as strategically and valuable.

Some examples of collaboration in performance improvement work include:
- effective listening to better understand value from the perspective of your stakeholders and to understand the context of the performance challenge or opportunity
- driving teamwork that recognizes and rewards achievement of group and organizational goals, rather than individual performance in the spirit of competition
- establishing partnerships to team up with other groups in the organization and reduce silo work
- supporting and committing to group decisions to foster teamwork and shared accountabilities for performance improvement efforts.

The skills described here embody the questions we ask ourselves and others, which in turn shape our view of specific situations and the world in general. Asking the right questions is one of the most important things you can do in your work. Yet, preparation and practice in asking the right questions seems hard to find for L&D professionals. Let's turn our focus to the art of skill of asking questions.

Asking the Right Questions

Research indicates that children ask hundreds of questions a day, but as we get older, this number consistently drops. Part of this has to do with our education system, which in turn shapes societal norms and expectations. We are asked to sit quietly and are rewarded for having the answers, rather than asking questions. The number of questions we ask appears to significantly diminish by the time we are in middle school, and interestingly, some research has also found that student creativity and engagement also significantly plummets around this time (Craft, Gardner, and Claxton 2015). While it's difficult to say whether there is cause and effect and in which direction it runs, the trend of asking fewer questions as we get older is troubling.

Deborah Meier is an award-winning pioneer known for her radical model for schools designed to foster inquiry and for her work with Central Park East schools in New York City. Meier tells the story of a third grader who described what was different about her school: "you are interested in what we don't know, not just what we do know" (Berger 2016). Meier believed that instead of just shoving information at kids, schools should teach them how to make sense of that information, so they could interpret it and figure out what to do with it. Her main concern was with developing children into critical thinkers and problem solvers who could add value to a democratic society. Consequently, she outlined five habits of mind, which served as the foundation of her school philosophy and approach:

- **Evidence:** How do we know what is true or false? What evidence counts?
- **Viewpoint:** How might this look if we looked at it from a different direction
- **Connection:** Is there a pattern? Have we seen something like this before?
- **Conjecture:** What if it were different?
- **Relevance:** Why does this matter?

These habits happen to be a succinct way to synthesize the essential skills described in the previous section. You will see them embodied in the strategic alignment process described throughout this book.

Of course, the art of questioning has been around for thousands of years. The philosopher Socrates developed the Socratic Method, which is a form of cooperative dialogue between individuals, based on asking and answering the right questions to stimulate critical thinking, and to draw out assumptions and ideas. Socrates is known as one of the great educators in history, and he taught by asking questions with the purpose of challenging accuracy and completeness of thinking in a way that moved people toward a valuable and ultimate goal.

There are various lines of Socratic style questions that can help us have substantive conversations with our clients and generate shared conclusions. These questions are meant to challenge what people think they know from a collaborative perspective.

As with any tool, they can be used well or used poorly. They should be asked from a place of "help me understand" rather than "I don't believe you," so appropriate delivery, wording, and pacing should be considered, especially when asking "why" questions. Table 1-1 provides six different types of questioning—conceptual clarification questions; probing assumptions; probing rationale, reasons, and evidence; probing viewpoints and perspectives; and probing implications and consequences—as well as their purpose and examples of each.

Table 1-1. Types of Socratic Questions

Type	Purpose	Examples
Conceptual Clarification Questions	Help others think deeper about the underlying concepts of their arguments	• Why are you saying that? • What exactly does that mean? • How does this relate to what we have been talking about? • What do we already know about this? • Can you give me an example? • Are you saying . . . or . . . ? • Can you rephrase that?
Probing Assumptions	Help others think about the unquestioned beliefs that underlie their arguments	• What else could we assume? • Are you assuming . . . ? • How did you choose those assumptions? • Please explain why . . . ? • How can you verify or disprove that assumption? • What would happen if . . . ? • Do you agree or disagree with . . . ?
Probing Rationale, Reasons, and Evidence	Help others think through their reasoning rather than assume it is a given	• Why is that happening? • How do you know this? • Can you give me an example of that? • What do you think causes that? • What evidence is there to support what you are saying?
Probing Viewpoints and Perspectives	Help you challenge particular viewpoints	• Another way of looking at this is. . . . Does this seem reasonable? • What alternative ways of looking at this are there? • Why is . . . necessary? • Who benefits from this? • What is the difference between . . . and . . . ? • Why is it better than . . . ? • What are its strengths and weaknesses? • What if you compared . . . and . . . ? • How could you look at this another way?
Probing Implications and Consequences	Help you consider logical implications that can be foreseen	• Then what would happen? • What are the consequences of that assumption? • How could . . . be used to . . . ? • What are the implications of . . . ? • How does . . . affect . . . ? • How does this fit with what we learned before? • Why is it important?

Keep the following guidelines in mind as you consider what questions must be asked:

- **Directness.** Consider how straightforward you want to be about your questions. Keep in mind who you are asking and what the appropriate way to ask the question is.
- **Open versus closed.** Consider what you want to know. Asking closed yes or no questions will give you limited information. Asking open-ended questions will allow the respondent to expand, explain, and even shape subsequent questions. While closed-ended questions can be helpful in confirming facts, they should be used sparingly, as they typically constrain you to narrow information.
- **Approach and tactics.** The value is not just in what questions you ask, but how you ask the questions. Over time, you want to develop your ability to combine different types of questions that complement each other well. Consider starting with probing questions that help you gather facts and perceptions (mainly descriptive). Then continue with probing questions that help you analyze the underlying assumptions, logics, and evidence. Finish with questions that help you begin to think about the future and alternatives.
- **Questions to avoid.** While you want to use a range of questions to broaden your understanding of the issues, there are some questions that you want to steer clear of. Avoid leading questions, which plant a seed in the respondent. You also want to avoid asking multiple questions at once, because the respondent will end up tackling the one he wants to answer, while ignoring the others. Finally, you also want to minimize direct "why" questions. This takes some care, as "why" is a critical question to understand contributing factors and root causes. But you also need to be thoughtful about how you ask these questions to avoid appearing critical or combative. Other ways of asking "why" questions include "tell me more about" or "what do you think are the reasons for. . .?"

Performance improvement practitioners help their organizations more through the questions they ask than through the answers they provide. This does not necessarily mean that you don't ever have useful answers, but rather that there is much value in the collaborative inquiry you engage stakeholders in to help them leverage their understanding of their situation and organizational culture. Through this process, you also gain their trust and a shared understanding of the important organizational issues. When you help them expand their view of the options they have, they are more likely to recognize the way forward for themselves, with an increased motivation and trust to move in that direction.

Asking the right questions is integral to strategic alignment—to collecting useful evidence about what is working well, what is not working well, why, what the priorities are, and how they should be addressed. Your choice of questions will lead you in a specific direction, and if you limit the scope of the questions, you will be limited by the information you acquire. An example of limiting your scope is to focus on isolated elements of individual performance, rather than focusing on the organizational system.

Toward a Focus on the Organizational System

The conventional view of L&D professionals has focused almost exclusively on employee learning without enough thought given to the performance context of the employee. While there may have been an analysis of important factors such as learner characteristics and preferences, and even the systematic design of the training itself, including knowledge testing to determine knowledge gains, there has been little alignment to the broader organizational context within which employees are expected to apply newly learned skills. This narrow focus misses opportunities to influence and evaluate transfer of learning to the workplace and gains in performance.

Over time, this view has expanded to an employee performance focus, although the preferred solution still appears to be training. This can be seen by an increased discourse on the "transfer of training" and in discussions about improved performance. While this shows some progress, it is unclear if the shift has fully manifested in practice. A true performance perspective requires you to look at the performance system, not the individual performer. Table 1-2 contrasts the traditional focus on employee learning to a performance alignment focus.

Table 1-2. Traditional View Versus Performance Alignment

Traditional View of L&D	Performance Alignment View of L&D
Changes in behavior are a function of individual knowledge, attitudes, and beliefs	Individual knowledge, attitudes, and beliefs are shaped by recurring patterns of behavioral interactions in the environment
Primary focus of solutions is the content of knowledge, attitudes, and beliefs—actual behavior will follow	Primary focus of solutions should be behavior—attitudes and ideas should be shaped to support behaviors
Performance can be isolated and changed individually	Performance of the organizational system has a greater effect on the individual than that of the individual on the system
The target of change should be at the individual person (knowledge and skills)	The target of change should be at the organization level (roles, responsibilities, communication, and feedback flows)

By conducting a thorough diagnosis of the performance context and the problem at hand before picking a solution, you will have a greater chance of figuring out the best solution. But improving organizational performance does not begin and end with deciding on the right solutions. It is part of a broader journey that consists of:

- baseline measures of performance (starting point)
- performance standards and targets (destination)
- viable alternatives based on key factors and criteria (best route and vehicles)
- evaluation framework (how to tell when we have arrived).

From a system view, you can see beyond individual employee performance and understand that you can't do much to influence their performance without addressing the system in which employees interact. It's important to remember that learning solutions are a drop in the bucket of performance improvement.

It is within this context that we present a detailed process for how to align sustainable performance improvement efforts to the organization's strategic objectives. We discuss examples specifically related to aligning traditional L&D programs to organizational priorities, as well as explore aligning broader organizational improvement initiatives in a variety of contexts. Chapter 2 provides a detailed discussion of strategic alignment, describing what it is, arguing why to do it, and introducing how to do it, which is then further detailed throughout the rest of the book.

Strategic Alignment

The term *strategic* is often thrown around in organizations, but few truly understand the term. If you are going to partner with stakeholders in applying a strategic approach to learning and talent development, you must have a clear understanding of what that means. Strategic alignment is the dynamic state of linking everything the organization uses, does, produces, and delivers to its strategic objectives. It allows the organization to optimize its resources (people, time, money) and processes for meeting its mission and making measurable progress toward its vision. There are many internal elements to consider when engaging in the process of strategic alignment, including systems, structure, staff, skills, finances, and shared values and practices.

Strategic alignment is not limited to the internal alignment or an organization's structure and resources to an organization's strategic objectives; it can also include alignment to its external environment (for example, government laws, environmental policies, customer needs, technology trends, economic environment, regulatory agencies, or peers or competitors). Ignoring these external factors can have catastrophic consequences for an organization. In fact, Roger Kaufman argues that true system thinking goes beyond the organization itself, and is instead anchored at the societal level (2004, 2006).

Another dimension of strategic alignment emphasizes the importance of strategic partnerships or alliances. Further efficiencies and even innovation can be realized by partnerships with organizations that share similar objectives. Strategic alliances can also be useful when one organization possesses a capability that can benefit another, but the other does not want to develop its internal capability. Organizations can benefit by leveraging their strengths to add greater value to customers, employees, communities, and shareholders.

The process presented in this book focuses primarily on the first two dimensions of alignment; however, it does not necessarily exclude the third. Creating fit among organizational activities in relationship to external and internal environments is synonymous with strategic alignment. Successful organizations do not waste time, energy, or money on activities that are not essential to their success. Strategically oriented organizations connect action to a value-added purpose that interacts with and reinforces other activities. Such organizations carefully consider their strategy—specifically, how to deploy their resources to the processes that will have the greatest impact on their strategic priorities.

When it comes to strategic alignment and performance, the purpose and scope of the L&D function may be viewed from different orientations. From one perspective, developing workforce performance encompasses the design and delivery of performance support products and services—for example, producing and delivering the products and services internal clients request. From another perspective, it encompasses a strategic role in organizations dedicated to aligning the workforce to execute organizational priorities. These two approaches represent how the function chooses to approach change and, in turn, strategic alignment in organizations.

As facilitators, designers, and managers of human performance in organizations, L&D has a choice about the contributions it seeks to make and their consequences. The distinction between these two choices is an important one because it affects the work you do, how you do it, and what results are accomplished. Learning and development can choose to react to performance problems by providing relevant solutions (often self-diagnosed by the internal client), or it can proactively influence human and organizational performance by systemically aligning to strategic priorities and opportunities. Both approaches are critical and complementary, but the distinction must be clearly understood.

To progress from transactional to consultative approaches, L&D professionals must break conventional reactive practices and instead align their goals, practices, culture, and expertise to support the organization's strategic goals. They can and should be seen as facilitators and stewards of strategy by developing the knowledge and skills of organizational members and the required performance support that delivers valued outputs. It is with this perspective and associated efforts that L&D members may gain their seat at the decision-making table and participate in strategic choices by bringing in the critical human performance system vantage point (Kraiger, McLinden, and Casper 2004). The consequence of this approach is the creation and capitalization of novel opportunities that may not have otherwise been found.

In addition to proactively planning and designing your future and how to arrive there, you also have a role in addressing deviations from plans, targets, standards, and norms. When these deviations or gaps occur, you must provide solutions to remedy them—this is the reactive part of your work. Even if you are diligent about front-end assessment, you are still being asked to react or respond to a perceived problem.

Reactive alignment is not bad; in fact, it is a critical part of performance management. You monitor current performance against performance plans, and how you handle discrepancies between the two is what performance management is about. L&D professionals have a critical role in problem solving with internal clients such as managers. You have a responsibility to ensure proper alignment between the solutions you provide and the identified performance problems. There is a wide range of tools for doing this based on performance measurement and a system perspective, including performance assessments and analysis, design, implementation support and change management, and performance tracking and evaluation that offer feedback to the system for continual improvement.

This book addresses both proactive and reactive alignment. Chapters 3, 4, and 5 provide a detailed set of processes for effectively and efficiently solving human performance problems, and ensuring strategic alignment of chosen solutions. Chapter 7 helps create and capitalize on greater opportunities by providing a validated tool to assess, design, and evaluate the strategic alignment of L&D as an organizational functional unit. First, let's more clearly define the distinction between problems and opportunities

Problems Versus Opportunities

In the performance improvement field, *problems* and *opportunities* are often used in the same breath, without a clear explanation of how they are related. A pervasive view is that the difference between a problem and an opportunity comes down to your mindset. If you're optimistic you see opportunities and if you're pessimistic you see problems. This view assumes that both desirable (opportunities) and undesirable (problems) events can produce comparable possibilities. Moreover, this view also assumes that if you simply spend more time on an analysis, you will find more opportunities than problems.

However, the time spent on analysis isn't the only thing that influences whether you find problems or opportunities; it also depends on what you are looking for. If your focus is on the discrepancy or deviation of something from a preset target, you are essentially looking to identify a problem, and it is possible that an appropriate solution would bring about favorable or desired consequences. If you are focused on observing favorable events or occurrences that could drive you toward a desired end, you are likely to find opportunities, whether in the presence of a problem or not. In a book about strategic performance improvement and alignment, it is critical to provide a thoughtful definition of the two.

Within this book, an opportunity is a set of circumstances that makes it possible to do and accomplish something. These circumstances—or occasions—are perceived as positive and can drive us toward a desirable goal. An example of an externally driven opportunity includes lifestyle or economic changes of customers that may make it possible for the organization to offer them a better and still affordable level of service. Another example might include changes in government policies or regulations that can provide favorable circumstances for an organization to change the way in which it offers services, targets new customers, or serves existing customers through new services. Internally driven opportunities may include changes in technology that allow employees to do their work in new and improved ways, leading to time and cost efficiencies not possible before. Changes in leadership is another common type of opportunity because it introduces greater possibilities of getting external unbiased perspectives that can lead to new types of programs and initiatives, and propel the organization toward its desired ends.

Opportunities can arise from any direction at any point. External opportunities can be identified after an analysis of strengths, weaknesses, opportunities, and threats, or simply by observing and reflecting on occurrences and circumstances relevant to a goal of interest. Internal opportunities can be found in just about any organizational change (planned or unplanned), as they may offer the possibilities to drive performance in faster, cheaper, better, or more innovative ways.

A problem, within this book, is a deficit or discrepancy between an existing state and a desired state. Problems are deviations from targets or standards, which require a solution to overcome them. Problems typically have multiple root causes and solution alternatives. However, significant challenges and negative consequences can arise when problems are insufficiently defined or ignored, and instead people jump to solution selection. In many instances, what appear to be relatively minor problems can be just the tip of the iceberg, with serious negative consequences if not examined more carefully.

Initial communication from managers to learning and development might very likely be a request for a solution rather than a request to help solve a problem. L&D functions that respond to requests (for example, training) without first defining the problem through reliable and valid evidence—and then aligning problem resolution to strategic priorities—risk wasting resources, hurting the performance of the organization, and consequently, reducing the total strategic value of L&D support. This is not to suggest that you cannot or should not incorporate design thinking from the start; instead, defining the problem first is critical for solution selection and design. Design thinking is about creating innovative ideas to solve problems or discover new opportunities. Of course, you have to make sure you are solving the right problem.

Is Strategic Alignment a Worthy Pursuit?

Aligning what your organization uses, does, produces, and delivers reduces wasted effort, time, and money that can lead to poor performance, as well as demotivation, decreased engagement, and even cynicism among organizational members. Employees who have longer institutional memories can be particularly discouraged by the parade of organizational solutions that have come and gone, only to raise false hopes of making things better and end in disappointment. After a while, employees no longer believe their workplace can become better, lose confidence in their leaders, and perhaps even check out of the organization—no longer willing to put in the extra effort to help make future initiatives a success.

From a system view, you have to understand the context within which your target population works and is expected to implement the learned skills. You also have to understand why they should be trained in the first place:

- What problem are you trying to solve?
- How is a selected solution going to solve that problem?
- What is the ultimate goal for the proposed program?

Then, you need understand what training content is required; how the training should be delivered given learner characteristics and the performance context; and what support or changes to their environment will be required for learners to be able to use the skills and realize any potential benefits.

Clark and Estes (2000, 48) note that highly regarded research groups who surveyed performance improvement solutions found "a huge gap between what we think we accomplish and what scientific analyses say we accomplished." Citing findings from the National Academy of Science, the National Research Council, and other independent groups, they suggest that the majority of organizational change initiatives are quickly abandoned; transfer of performance solutions show that even though they may work once, they almost never work in other organizational contexts because they aren't evaluated; a third of performance feedback strategies fail, and another third make performance worse; and successful performance improvement solutions do exist, but they are rarely integrated into the commonly used performance solutions.

Organizations experience many failed initiatives, and these failures are the result of many interrelated factors. Among them, our experience tells us that two major categories of factors that contribute to misalignment are:

- **Fit between perceived problem and selected solution:** This occurs when there is a disconnect between what the solution can deliver and the actual needs of the target population or organization. This is often the case when solutions are selected before the problem is clearly defined through reliable and valid evidence.
- **Fit between the selected solution and the implementation context:** Even when the chosen solution has a strong potential to solve a problem, poor or nonexisting tactics for implementing the solution and managing the change prevent the solution from delivering what it was intended to deliver.

While it may sound simplistic to lump most of the reasons for failed organizational solutions into two categories, it is important to reiterate that each category is composed of many interrelated factors, and often both categories interact to contribute to failed organizational initiatives.

Misalignment of Problems and Selected Solutions

Some organizational programs fail because they are chosen as solutions in search of problems. In other words, the decision to implement the program or solution was made before the problem was clearly defined or needs properly assessed. Needs assessment is an approach to problem solving, which is focused primarily on defining problems and generating suggested courses of action (Kaufman 2000; Kaufman and Guerra-López 2013). A needs assessment is most useful when it is conducted before a potential solution is identified to ensure that it is driven by evidence of its appropriateness and relevance to strategic objectives and priorities. This is consistent with research conducted by Nutt (2008, 2007), who found that a discovery approach to decision making (one that follows a logical and evidence-based approach to solution identification) was more successful than an idea imposition approach (one that adheres to extreme pragmatism and attempts to rationalize or make sense of an initial idea, without evidence of its potential utility, and sometimes unconsciously disregarding evidence to the contrary). These findings were supported across various conditions, no matter the urgency, importance, resources, initial support, decision maker, sector, or type of decision.

The issue of choosing one approach over the other is not as simple as it may seem. Research in social psychology and behavioral economics has exposed a long list of decision-making biases that may not be visible to decision makers and may be rooted in our thinking processes. They can minimize mental effort and avoid difficult trade-offs by relying on experience, hunch, gut feelings, and convenient rules of thumb. While these can help you function more efficiently, they also bring significant risks. Table 2-1 provides a brief overview of some of the cognitive biases that may get in the way of making sound choices about your performance improvement solutions. As you can see, a needs assessment can give you a false sense of confidence. As with any tool, a needs assessment can be applied effectively or ineffectively. For instance, in learning and development a needs assessment is applied ineffectively when you start with a training needs assessment. A training needs assessment, as the name implies, focuses on training needs and signifies an idea-imposition approach, where you have already decided that training is the best idea, and any data you collect simply serve to justify your conclusions. A training needs assessment may help you understand the profiles and preferences of your prospective trainees, but it is unlikely you will uncover performance issues unrelated to training. If you don't see the entire picture, you will miss it, and yet, some L&D professionals are happy and confident to deliver training anyway.

Of course, this is not to suggest that training is never the answer. In many cases training is not only effective, but essential and even legally required. Instead, this is to remind you to be cautious of assuming training is the primary solution to most performance problems. You should also be wary of assuming that just because your department or job title includes "learning," you are exclusively bound to deliver learning solutions.

Table 2-1. Decision-Making Biases

Bias	Description	Examples of Measures to Reduce Their Effect
When We Are Defining the Problem		
Anchoring Bias	We fixate on initial information and fail to adequately adjust based on subsequent information.	• Do not automatically accept the initial problem frame. • Consider how the framing of the problem affected any recommended solutions.
Confirmation Bias	We seek information that confirms or reaffirms our preconceptions, and discard or even fail to see information that contradicts them.	• Be honest with yourself about your motives, assumptions, and preconceived notions. • Determine whether your questions are balanced in breadth and depth or leave room for disproving your initial hypothesis.
Availability Bias	We base judgments on information that is readily available—the easier to recall, the more importance we attribute to it.	• Before looking at what information is available, consider what questions should be asked and answered when defining the problem. Then see what information is available and what information is missing.
When We Are Considering Solutions		
Overconfidence Bias	We tend to be too optimistic about our probabilities of being right.	• Consider extreme and honest scenarios of what could go wrong with your choices. • Seek critical input about the logic of your choices and accept that you could be wrong.
Status Quo Bias	We tend to be protective of the way things are now.	• Remember the objectives; is maintaining the status quo is the best way to achieve them? • The status quo is not the only option; come up with other alternatives.
Risk Aversion Bias	We tend to choose a sure thing over what we perceive to be a risky option.	• Be honest in your estimation of the risks by focusing on the evidence and deemphasizing unfounded fear. • Ask others for honest input on the potential risks and benefits, without biasing them with your own opinions.
When We Look Back at Our Selected Solutions		
Escalation of Commitment Bias (also known as the sunk-cost bias)	We want to stay with a decision even when there is clear evidence that it is wrong because we already invested so much time, energy, and face.	• Seek input from those who were not involved in the initial decision and have no vested interest. • Cultivate an organizational culture where mistakes are seen as learning opportunities rather than failures.
Hindsight Bias	We tend to falsely believe that after an outcome is known, we would have predicted it correctly.	• Conduct an honest evaluation of the obtained results, as well as their contributing factors. • Reflect on the process you took for framing the problem and selecting the solution.

The term *needs assessment* is often used interchangeably with other terms such as *performance assessment, front-end assessment, performance analysis,* and *diagnosis.* It's critical to understand that a needs assessment is simply a framework for gathering data about specific gaps in performance results so you can be sure there is a real and measurable performance gap or opportunity to address. For example, are you experiencing a consistent gap between your current sales figures and your target sales figures? Do you have a gap in the percentage of customer issues that are successfully resolved during their first call? Have you experienced an increase in your error rate? Has the number of customer complaints significantly increased? Has the rate of infections in your hospital increased beyond an acceptable level? Has the average length of stay in the hospital increased beyond your target? This is critical to strategic alignment.

While defining needs in terms of performance gaps is necessary to solve the problem, it is not sufficient. In addition to defining the performance problem, you also need to understand why these gaps exist. Have you ever walked into a physician's office and asked for a specific medication or drug and had a doctor or nurse say, "Sure! How much of it do you want? Do you want the liquid form or the pill form? Do you want enough for all your friends? Do you like it flavored?" What do you suppose most people would think if they witnessed this? Would they question the physician's competence? What about their ethics? Their motivations?

Just because someone asks questions, it doesn't mean that they are analyzing the problem or getting any closer to understanding the issues. While the doctor scenario may seem silly, it is a clear illustration of how futile and perhaps even dangerous it can be to focus your questions and information gathering on arbitrary issues. A useful analysis focuses on understanding the problem by uncovering root causes and contributing factors, how those factors relate to one another, and what organizational or broader system structures and routines are maintaining the problem. Yes, asking questions is critical, but to gather useful information, you must ask the right questions.

Take the process of a medical diagnosis, for example, in which the physician examines your symptoms. Based on the physician's medical knowledge and experience about how the body works, and factors typically contributing to the observed symptoms, the physician then investigates factors to confirm or refute the initial hypothesis. This may involve further questioning and analyses guided by the initial hypothesis. At this stage, the physician's questions are not about what treatment you prefer (for example, what quantity and how much of the solution you want), they are about getting a complete picture of the problem. Once the physician has the information she needs to make a well-supported diagnosis, only then will she give you her recommendation for treatment. This doesn't necessarily have to take a long time, but due diligence is critical. Certainly, there is a place to discuss your preferences, but only after all viable options have been identified based on the causal factors.

Organizational solutions must be thoughtfully aligned to the key factors of the problem you are trying to solve. Keep in mind that the overwhelming majority of performance problems are a product of circular patterns of events at the organizational level. For example, your data indicate a dip in sales for the sales team, so you quickly jump into solution mode and tackle the problem in two key ways: First, you retrain the sales team to make sure they have the best knowledge in the industry, and second, you enhance the incentives for meeting sales targets. However, you still don't see a noticeable improvement in sales.

Why not? Well, you never asked the "why" question. That should have been asked immediately upon noticing the decreased sales figures. Asking why may have revealed that the trained staff do not have a chance to apply the "best industry knowledge" if their supervisors are communicating conflicting expectations, are not providing relevant feedback and coaching on the job, or are discouraging the sales team from applying those techniques once they are out of the training environment and back in front of the customer.

Misalignment of Selected Solutions and Implementation

Clearly defining the problem, identifying contributing factors, and selecting proper solutions provides a strong foundation for improving performance, but other factors can still stop improvement efforts. Properly implementing improvement initiatives is critical to success and cannot be undermined. In fact, a key challenge for leaders and other individuals charged with a role in the organization's improvement and sustainability is implementing planned organizational changes. A growing body of research suggests that the specific behaviors of those leading the implementation can affect the success or failure of chosen solutions (Berson and Avolio 2004; Bommer, Rich, and Rubin 2005).

There are many models for managing the implementation of organizational initiatives (also known as change management). However, at its core effective organizational change implementation involves three key phases: communicating the change, mobilizing others to support the change, and monitoring the implementation of change. Yet, as we have seen from previous discussions, any model, theory, or process can vary greatly depending on who is implementing it and how it is being implemented.

Communicating the Change

The basis for implementing organizational change is effectively communicating the need for change with organizational members. People must understand why they are being asked to change their routines if they are going to buy into the process and help make the planned change a reality. Often, resistance arises when people don't understand what changes they are being asked to make and why they are being asked to make them. When they are kept in the dark, they develop an emotional reaction that stems from fear, anxiety, or stress associated with confusion and uncertainty. Change agents have to be cognizant of these potential reactions and take measures to address them by identifying who needs to know what, when, and how, and devising a communication plan for getting the right information into the right hands at the right time.

While this might seem like common sense, this step is often overlooked and the implementation of organizational initiatives moves forward without a communication plan that is carefully developed and faithfully executed. Consequently, organizational members are surprised when yet another change is implemented without their knowledge or input.

Mobilizing Others to Accept Change

Mobilizing others to adopt a new organizational initiative into their daily routines can be a tall order. People are inherently driven by their own objectives—professional and personal. Their perception of the desirability of new organizational initiatives will be influenced by these objectives, as well as their past experiences and perceived rewards (or negative consequences). Those who see the new initiative as a means of getting closer to reaching their objectives and interests will be more ready to adopt or help support the implementation of the change. Conversely, those who see the proposed change as a threat to their own interests and objectives are more likely to resist.

John Kotter (1995) proposed building a "coalition for change" to support the change process. This group is essentially charged with stewarding the change initiative through its various stages, and the quality of the group's composition is critical. Its members must be perceived as competent, credible, and influential, and be the right mix of leaders, managers, and frontline members. They must also be able to work together effectively to influence others to accept the change. The importance of leadership support and engagement with the change coalition cannot be overstated. Without leadership support, the coalition may not be able to counter any inevitable resistance to the change.

Mobilizing others to accept change takes more than influence from a change coalition, however. It also requires the redesign of organizational systems and processes to support organization members to adopt changes. Changes require a work environment conducive to those changes. For example, the implementation of a new sales process may require changes in the job description and incentive structure. A new job technique for staff may also require staff supervisors to provide timely coaching and feedback on the job. A change in how a job out in the field will be conducted may also require changes to the way that job is monitored and evaluated.

Monitoring the Implementation of Organizational Change

The point of establishing goals, objectives, and plans is to trigger momentum forward; otherwise, they're next to useless. This key step forward is implementing the steps you outlined in your plans, as required for reaching your goals and objectives. Monitoring implementation is a critical aspect of managing performance, whether it's people, programs, or organizations. Part of managing the change initiatives is to monitor whether people are performing the new routines or behaviors. This cannot be done by one change agent alone, or even by the change coalition. The approach to monitoring implementation should be articulated before the change is implemented. Clear metrics of progress should be identified, as well as how the data will be collected and used to make corrections or improvements along the way, and who will be responsible for what aspects. Without a clear process for improving throughout the process, you will end up with missed opportunities to ensure success.

This requires collaboration between change agents, leadership, managers, frontline employees, learning and development, and other relevant members of the organization. Monitoring is not a process for pointing fingers or finding blame; it is a mechanism for ensuring timely feedback reaches those who are enabled to adjust if goals are off-target. So, it must be presented and understood in this way, if it is going to be useful in ensuring that your selected initiatives deliver useful results.

Within this context, you want to make sure that the initiatives are having the intended effect on performance at various levels of the organization. So, monitoring the implementation of initiatives should be aligned to the organization's formal performance measurement and management systems. The role of measurement in management and strategic alignment is central and thus deserves careful discussion.

The Role of Measurement

Geary Rummler's work is the quintessential example of a performance improvement approach, as it is guided by two key questions: "What are the variables that measure the results desired? What variables must we manage to achieve those results?" (Brethower 2009, 18). A performance improvement approach takes a system approach to strategic assessment and alignment, evaluation, and management of human and organizational performance, as well as its external influence on clients and society (Guerra-López 2008). Performance measurement is a central mechanism in both assessment and evaluation. Initially, a needs assessment process provides a framework for measuring gaps and generating the performance data you require to make sound decisions about how to close these gaps. This allows you to align the right solutions to the right problems, and in turn, devise a plan for effectively implementing those solutions. You also monitor those solutions to measure progress toward desired results and generate feedback about what is working, what is not, and how to get back on track. And you measure and report the final results to ensure accountability for the resources consumed and the commitments made by those involved with the implementation. This then generates lessons learned and informs management of the direction of broader organizational change.

A performance improvement approach to learning and development centers on aligning the relevant performance measures of the results you seek and asking what variables must be managed to achieve those results. This will help ensure that what is measured, and in turn, what data are used and how they are used is based on shared values and beliefs about what is important and why. Without exploring the underlying assumptions of what measures are important, the measurement system can be misaligned and met with dissatisfaction or indifference among its prospective users.

Up to this point, this chapter has dealt with the conceptual framework for the process of aligning learning and talent development to organizational strategy and priorities that will be presented throughout the rest of this book. Let's conclude with an overview of the strategic alignment process.

The Four Alignment Levels

Roger Kaufman's Organizational Elements Model (OEM) has been a useful and respected framework for organizational alignment for decades (Kaufman 1998, 2000; Kaufman and Guerra-López 2013). Kaufman, as do we in this book, makes a fundamental distinction between means and ends: *Ends* are why the organization exists to accomplish and deliver, while *means* are how it goes about doing that. *Means* include the processes, programs, projects, activities, and resources that the organization uses and does to accomplish the desired ends. This book adopts the general OEM framework, and adapts it such that the three levels of ends (outcomes, outputs, and products) are defined as:

- **Value-Add:** Long-term organizational results that ultimately benefit clients and society, often stated in a vision that describes the ideal state for those you serve (clients and external society) and is associated with a strategic level of planning. The timeline for the achievement of strategic aims is definitively long term because it represents a continuous journey toward an ideal. Success is best interpreted in terms of progress toward that ideal, rather than exclusively as the attainment of that ideal.
- **Organizational:** Results that specify the specific contributions of the organization toward that vision, usually stated in terms of an organizational mission. The timeline to achieve the specific targets set for these results can take five years (a typical strategic planning cycle) or longer (a longer—and

often more realistic—strategic horizon). This is the level of focus for much of what might be considered the conventional view of strategic planning.

- **Operational:** The building-block objectives, perhaps at the department, unit, team, or individual level, that allow you to reach the organizational mission. In some settings such as the military, operations are used to describe not only the building block results, but also the processes used to produce them. Timelines for these results tend to be annual, and broken down even further into quarters and months depending on what is appropriate for the given result.

In the OEM framework, the other two elements of the means are processes and inputs. *Processes* include anything the organization does to accomplish its operational, tactical, and strategic results; *inputs* are the resources consumed for carrying out the processes and all other organizational activities and efforts. One critical idea to strategic alignment is that your chosen processes, activities, and efforts must be driven by the results you want, rather than the other way around. You do not want to choose means (for example, a training program) and assume that the desired results—enhanced performance or changed behavior—will automatically materialize. So, you must align *how* the work gets done to *what* results must be accomplished.

In the context of strategically aligning learning and talent development, the remaining alignment level can be called learning. Will Thalheimer (2016, 36) offers a useful way to look at learning alignment. The Training Maximizers Model is a seven-element model to help people "begin thinking about what effective performance training looks like":

1. valid credible content
2. engaging learning events
3. support for basic understanding
4. support for decision-making competence
5. support for long-term remembering
6. support for application of learning
7. support for perseverance in learning.

This causal framework for learning effectiveness gives us a lens through which we can view alignment within this level.

We then define this level specifically as being focused on what human performers know, do, and how they do it; specifically, their knowledge, skills, and behaviors. This level is not quite a result in the sense of the definitions offered previously, but it is still observable and measurable. This is a core fabric of organizational alignment because it facilitates the work that must be done within the organization to deliver valuable results at the operational, organizational, and value-add levels.

The Strategic Alignment Process

The strategic alignment process integrates all these essential elements and considerations into a structured yet flexible process for ensuring that your talent development efforts clearly align to strategic objectives and generate useful feedback for decision making and hard evidence of your contributions to the organization's success. The process rests on a performance measurement backbone that connects needs assessment, monitoring, and evaluation as essential performance management and improvement tools. It offers a pragmatic way to establish effective partnerships with your stakeholders through a series of key questions and activities that help ensure you have the information needed to make the best decisions possible.

The strategic alignment process comprises four phases, which are all equally important and require specific outputs to successfully complete the other stages (Figure 2-1).

Figure 2-1. The Strategic Alignment Process

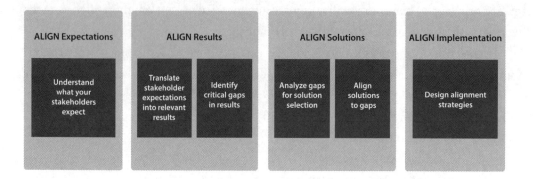

Phase 1. ALIGN Expectations

Phase one helps performance improvement practitioners gain an understanding of the expectations, wants, and perceived performance needs from various stakeholder vantage points. These stakeholders include the person that made the original request for assistance and those who will affect or be affected by the selected solutions, which could include top leadership, frontline supervisors, staff, or other functional unit representatives relevant to the focus of this work.

With a calibration of these perspectives, you will gain an understanding of what is or will be driving stakeholder decision making, assumptions, and satisfaction. In a sense, this is the beginning of creating and managing organizational change—as people become engaged in the process, their views shape the focus of improvement efforts to be done. Ultimately, this helps the performance improvement team have a more complete view of the issues and some of the factors that may affect their efforts and the successful implementation of proposed organizational initiatives.

Phase 2. ALIGN Results

Phase two helps you identify measurable gaps in results at various levels. First, the performance improvement team works with stakeholders to translate wants and expectations into the current and desired levels of results in learning, performance, value-added contribution to clients and community, and other strategic consequences that affect organizational sustainability. Many organizational members find it challenging to articulate their wants in terms of specific and measurable performance results, so the performance improvement team can be instrumental in aligning wants and valuable results.

These results are linked to the strategic priorities of the organization and related functions, operations, processes, and other core elements. This is the foundation of the measurement framework and provides the focus of your data collection through relevant performance indicators. Data are collected to determine the critical gaps between current and desired results. These priority gaps are the foundation for further analysis, recommendation of solutions, and implementation plans.

Phase 3. ALIGN Solutions

In phase three, the performance improvement team focuses on the deliberate analysis of priority gaps. Now that you know exactly what problems need to be solved and which gaps addressed, it is critical to understand each of those problems. What are the contributing factors? How do those contributing factors affect each other? What elements of the environment are perpetuating these recurrent patterns? The answers will provide the team with a thorough understanding of what potential solutions should be able to do and deliver.

The process of identifying alternative solutions should be collaborative, and include input from stakeholders, beginning with identifying relevant and useful criteria for selecting improvement solutions. This helps ensure that the process of identifying alternatives and selecting the best solutions is not only driven by evidence, but also well informed by the individual needs of the organization's culture and resources. The alternatives are ultimately weighed to select the solutions that are most likely to offer the best payoffs in the most resource-efficient ways.

Phase 4. ALIGN Implementation

Phase four relates to critical success factors for effective implementation of your proposed organizational improvement initiatives to ensure successful execution, integration, and sustainability. Implementation includes the specific strategies for driving the transfer of L&D programs from an instructional environment to a performance environment. Thoughtful change management strategies that include defining who needs to be informed about what, when, and how, and how to gain useful input about other issues should be considered for implementation.

Mobilization strategies that you must align to effectively implement your improvement initiatives should also be defined. Should a core group or change coalition be formed to support the change? If so, who will be involved and in what ways? Mobilization strategies may also include defining implications for job descriptions, feedback mechanisms, performance evaluation, and process redesigns. Finally, a clear monitoring plan to track the progress of improvement initiatives must be defined, and should include what data must be tracked, how frequently will data be collected, who should use it and when, and how to use the data for corrective or improvement actions.

As we work through the four phases of the SAP throughout the rest of the book, we will follow a case study of our colleague, Kai, an internal organization development consultant and fellow performance improvement practitioner.

Case Study Introduction

Kai works on performance improvement initiatives as an internal organization development consultant at InsCo1, a midsized financial services organization. Kai's typical day includes consulting with stakeholders in the planning of initiative design, delivery, and implementation and then designing, delivering, and implementing those solutions.

The Request
Kai received a call from Jessie, an operations manager who oversees the claims department at InsCo1. Jessie began by describing the lack of teamwork and high turnover on the claims team. She then requested a team-building training session to boost morale. Kai agreed to meet the following week.

Typically, Kai would begin planning for a conversation about the design and implementation of the team-building solution Jessie requested. This was important for retaining a good working relationship with Jessie, because Kai did not want to "turn business away" by rejecting her request.

However, Kai also wanted the L&D department to be more strategically aligned to the business—there had to be a way to have a good working relationship with Jessie, keep the business, and work toward better alignment to the business. Kai decided to handle the meeting a little differently this time.

The Research
Kai set out to identify the mission, vision, and goals of the organization to gain an understanding of where InsCo1 is today and where it wants to go in the future.
- **Vision:** Creating secure futures
- **Mission:** To become the most trusted insurance provider of all our stakeholders and shareholders

- **Goals:**
  - Fully integrate InsCo1 with newly acquired InsCo2 by year 2020
  - Reduce annual voluntary turnover of all operations positions by 7 percent by year 2021
  - Zero fines by external regulators every year
  - Achieve strong, very strong, or superior credit ratings every reporting period
  - Improve reputation as a trusted insurance provider

To learn more about the work environment at InsCo1, Kai continued to research the organization. Kai learned that the organization employs 5,000 professionals working across five companies within the United States. InsCo1 recently acquired one of those five companies, InsCo2. The company values, which were documented on the corporate website and on posters in the break rooms, were:

- customer-driven
- performance-based
- open and continuous communication
- teamwork.

The website also featured a message from the CEO noting the organization's "execution-based culture," which, to the CEO, represented a focus on execution and getting it done right the first time.

Kai was also familiar with the claims department and how it was working to integrate its work with the work of the newly acquired company. Using this information, Kai set out a game plan to learn more about the performance challenges the claims department was experiencing. This meeting would be part of the first phase of alignment: ALIGN Expectations.

ALIGN Expectations

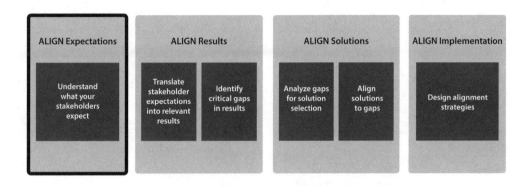

No matter how unified an organization is, its members may not always share expectations about what it should be doing or how it should go about doing it. L&D professionals may increase the success of their performance improvement work by knowing and thinking through what their clients want to achieve and what they expect will happen once they've achieved it. While it's safe to assume all stakeholders want to solve a problem plaguing performance, they often have different views about the actual problem, and different expectations about what the solution will look and feel like. Until you understand these expectations and define success, you are setting yourself up for disappointment—and misalignment. This is why aligning expectations is the first phase of the strategic alignment process.

The ALIGN Expectations phase is your opportunity to uncover your stakeholders' expectations of value—their wants, preferences, priorities, and perspectives—and to synergize these perspectives to ensure that you can facilitate positive and meaningful returns. Table 3-1 presents some objectives to accomplish and activities to help you meet them.

> Kai began applying the strategic alignment process skills by gaining an understanding of Jessie's expectations and what was driving her decisions and assumptions. Like most everyone at this company, Jessie wanted this project to be successful, so Kai considered how she would define success and the results for which she may be accountable.

Table 3-1. ALIGN Expectations: Objectives and Activities

Objectives to Accomplish	Activities Designed to Meet the Objectives
• Gain an understanding of the expectations, wants, and perceived performance needs from various stakeholder vantage points. • Gain an understanding of what is or will be driving stakeholder decision making, assumptions, and satisfaction from various stakeholder vantage points.	• Conduct discovery meetings with your initial requestor and other stakeholders. • Calibrate the various perspectives.
• Gain information that deepens your understanding of the issues and factors that may affect your efforts. • Gain an understanding of the performance context.	• Map the described performance problems throughout the organizational levels. • Identify alignment level of the work request.
• Set the stage for building and developing collaborative working relationships with your stakeholders.	• Establish partnerships, gain commitment, and establish roles and responsibilities for your discovery team.
• Conduct an ongoing reflection of your work.	• Review the ALIGN Expectations checklist to assess your performance.

Understanding Stakeholders

Understanding stakeholders and their interests is a critical entry point for L&D professionals to strengthen their strategic value propositions. If you don't understand their perspective and priorities, it will be difficult for you to help. Stakeholders regularly place competing demands on the organization's finite resources. Whether the resources are financial, effort, or time, different stakeholders will disagree about where and how they should be used. Therefore, it is important to keep in mind that behind any stakeholder decision, there are unique and perhaps narrow considerations about resource allocation.

Depending on the stakeholder's position, what influences her decision might be somewhat different. For example, the higher up the organizational chart you go, the more a manager is accountable for overarching organizational results, and the more receptive she is likely to be about addressing the "business" or "organizational result" issue. Thus you are likely to have more success in influencing this stakeholder by establishing how sharing resources (perhaps financial and time) for strategic alignment will help her attain the organizational results for which she is accountable.

Conversely, the closer an individual's accountability to a specific output or process, the greater his interest in ensuring that output or process is completed successfully. For example, a supervisor may be responsible for "calls answered on the first ring" or "number of patients whose co-pay was collected during office visit" or "widgets built." He is likely to be persuaded to share resources (perhaps time and effort) to get a closer look at actual performance gaps and root causes that will drive his team's performance. Organizational issues might be secondary for this supervisor, and so his views and priorities may look different from that of a manager.

Key Stakeholders

Thoughtfully identifying the key stakeholders involved in defining the problem and selecting or developing solutions is crucial because they will be instrumental in defining the scope of your efforts, as well as providing criteria for what constitutes an effective solution. So how do you determine your stakeholders?

Here, a stakeholder is any person with an interest or concern in the strategic alignment process. They can be managers, executives, employees, board members, strategic partners, funding entities, government, regulatory bodies, clients, or the community. Not all stakeholders have to be represented for every strategic alignment effort. Rather, depending on the focus and scope of the work, you will want to identify the appropriate stakeholders to include. Some of the initial tasks that can help identify relevant stakeholders include:

- Describe what appears to be the problem (based on the requestor's initial request).
- List what individuals or groups could be most affected by the problem (and potential solutions).
- List who can be most influential in helping drive change within the organization and how.
- List who might perceive the potential change as negative or threatening and why.
- Identify what potential barriers exist to enlisting their participation.

Using the stakeholder table (Table 3-2), Kai wrote some initial notes about the problem as described by Jessie, and then identified roles that could affect this project or be affected by it, as well as some initial ideas about potential limitations in carrying it out.

Another way to identify the key stakeholders for a particular initiative is to map them according to their relative influence and importance to the success of your strategic alignment project. To do this you can develop a matrix that helps you clearly identify the level of influence and importance of the various stakeholders (Figure 3-1).

Table 3-2. The Stakeholders

What is the initial problem?	Jessie, operations manager of the claims department, called to request a team-building course for claims associates. She described a lack of teamwork within the department and a high turnover of claims associates.
Which individuals or groups may affect or be affected by this project?	• Operations manager of the claims department • Claims associates • Policy owners • Insurance agents • Director of operations • Chief administrative officer
Who are the influential change agents? Describe their possible impact.	• Operations manager of claims department—the original requestor; motivated to improve teamwork and reduce turnover in the department • Insurance agents—agents are the primary customers of the company, and A-level agents may influence processes • Chief administration officer—with senior leadership support, the project is more likely to have access to resources.
Which individuals or groups may offer resistance to change? Why?	• Director of operations—the director is cautious to use resources for development purposes
What are potential barriers to adoption?	• The claims department is experiencing high volumes of work and is short staffed. Solutions must be integrated into the daily work of claims associates, as time away from the job will likely not be possible.

Figure 3-1. Stakeholder Mapping Tool

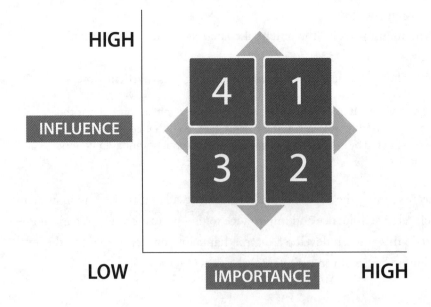

- **Quadrant one:** These stakeholders have high influence and high importance (for example, leadership, key managers, or supervisors) and need to be fully engaged on the strategic alignment process.
- **Quadrant two:** These stakeholders have high importance but low influence (for example, employees directly affected by the potential performance solution); however, they still need to be kept informed through appropriate education and communication.
- **Quadrant three:** These stakeholders have low influence and low importance; however, they should still be monitored and kept on board, as their relative position could change at any time. For example, these individuals could switch roles, and with that their influence within the organization may increase, as well as their potential for greater decision-making authority over resources. While many members of the organization may fall into this quadrant, you want to focus primarily on those that have the potential to influence others (whether formally or informally).
- **Quadrant four:** These stakeholders have high influence but low importance. They should be kept satisfied with appropriate approval and perhaps brought in as patrons or supporters who endorse the strategic alignment process of the potential performance improvement program. This will also lend credibility and influence to your findings and recommendations.

Later, this chapter provides more information about how to begin identifying the potential stakeholders with your primary requestor (the person who initially contacted you for your assistance). With an initial list of those stakeholders, you can determine their relative importance to the project to help map your approach with each.

It is critical to remember that the map is not static; stakeholders can change and thus move around with increasing or decreasing levels of importance and influence. Effectively managing stakeholder relationships is crucial to solving the wide range of issues facing organizations today. To successfully manage your relationships with stakeholders, consider the following guidelines:

- Acknowledge and actively monitor the concerns of stakeholders, and take their interests into account in decision making about alignment activities.
- Listen to and openly communicate with stakeholders about their respective concerns and contributions, as well as the risks they assume by committing their involvement.
- Recognize the interdependence of efforts and rewards among stakeholders, and attempt to achieve a fair distribution of the benefits and burdens, taking into account their respective risks and vulnerabilities.

The following section provides a discussion of stakeholder expectations and the wide range of factors that can affect where your stakeholders are in your stakeholder map, and in turn, better help you monitor and manage a trusting and productive relationship.

Stakeholder Expectations

In their bestselling book *Crucial Confrontations*, Kerry Patterson, Joseph Grenny, Ron McMillan, and Al Switzler argue that much of the conflict in the world—whether an organizational failure, a family breakdown, or national turmoil—is born from violated expectations. These expectations are typically violated because we assume others either know what we expect or we assume we know what others expect of us. We may think, "If they were smart, they would have figured out what I meant," or "If they cared enough, they would have looked into it further before jumping blindly into action," or "If they were proactive, they would have fixed the problem long ago and avoided the mess we are in today." We take for granted the uniqueness of our own perspectives and views, which are shaped by countless factors, and assume that what seems perfectly clear and real to us, seems just as obvious and logical to others. Of course, this—like much in life—is not a safe assumption.

The key is understanding the priorities for different stakeholders, what their underlying assumptions might be, and how collaborating in specific aspects of the strategic alignment process will help get them closer to achieving their goals. These efforts are aimed at making strategically aligned and collaborative decisions about the performance focus that is best suited for the situation presented to you by the requestor.

One common assumption held by stakeholders when requesting training or learning solutions is that if their people are not doing what they should be doing, they must not know how to do it, or they don't want to do it. Based on this stakeholder assumption, giving them more knowledge will remedy the situation. Many stakeholders may not have extensive education in or deep understanding of human and organizational behavior, and therefore may be unaware of the multitude of factors that affect human performance in the workplace. Consequently, they may not be able to recognize these factors in the workplace, or they may not have the vocabulary necessary to communicate what they have observed beyond, "people don't know how to . . ." or "people need to learn to . . ." Your ability to increase their awareness of other performance factors is important, as long as the approach is appropriate for each stakeholder group and without technical jargon.

Another stakeholder assumption might be that any type of up-front analysis or alignment will take more time than what they have available, and consequently, see it as a derailment to "taking action." However, delivering desired results efficiently and effectively is even more important than taking immediate action. Immediate action can introduce a false sense of confidence because you and the stakeholder think you are on your way to solving the problem when in fact you're not doing anything productive. Quick action should not be confused with efficiency, and certainly not with effectiveness. Effectiveness is about reaching the results you want, while efficiency is doing it better (for example, with the minimum required effort and energy). You need to help stakeholders clarify where they want to go and what it will take to get there. Only then are you in the position to recognize efficient and effective alternatives. Fortunately, you can satisfy the drive to take immediate action to remedy a problem, and still stay on the road of effectiveness and efficiency. You do this by clearly defining the decisions to be made, understanding the relevant questions to answer to make those decisions, and gathering the required information to make sound decisions. The strategic alignment process rests on this premise.

A third common stakeholder assumption is that the training department can only help with training. Some stakeholders may assume that your areas of expertise are purely in how to produce learning products or facilitate workshops. This stems from outdated practices in the field that have isolated learning and development from organizational realities and workforce challenges. As you establish yourself as a strategic partner through a demonstrable track record of delivering organizational results, this will change. At first, however, you will want to adopt a consultative problem-solving approach that helps stakeholders use critical thinking to better define key issues and appropriate solutions. You will earn credibility for understanding broader organizational issues and helping stakeholders select solutions that deliver results.

Factors Influencing Stakeholders Expectations

Stakeholders tend to come with their own interests. This doesn't necessarily mean that they harbor a hidden agenda. Rather, it means that given different positions in relation to the problems or opportunities that need to be addressed, they may share some priorities with organizational members and disagree on others based on their definition of value.

The concept of value in organizational settings is variable, but can be understood as something that has potential worth to stakeholders (Harrison and Wicks 2013; Kaplan and Norton 2004; Lukac and Frazier 2012). Perspectives of worth can vary, but also work together synergistically. For example, Glaveli and Karassavidou (2011) demonstrated how a manager may value effectiveness while employees may value job satisfaction, but these values are cohesive and realized in value to customers (for example, loyalty or perceptions of quality) and to organizational goals (for example, profitability). These various value preferences are often based on perception (Barney and Wright 1998) and derived from the "transactions, relationships and interactions," which influence perception of value (Harrison and Wicks 2013).

Others may take a contrasting approach, which Harrison, Bosse, and Phillips (2010) refer to as "satisficers." Satisficers take a passive approach to value creation by offering products that are based on assumptions about organizational needs or based on indirect or anecdotal evidence that informs which products are useful. Here, prioritized attention isn't given to proactive value creation, and, as such, opportunities for value creation go undetected. Creating strategic value for the L&D function is then the process of seeking requirements for shared value, identifying where those opportunities lie, and making ongoing adjustments to evolve strategically valuable and synergistic relationships.

With such variances in how stakeholders can interpret value, you can better understand how they define value through the choices they make: "We know from the basics of markets that people will tend to make choices that provide them the most value for what value they give up" (Harrison and Wicks 2013). With this understanding, a reasonable goal for learning and development is to provide "a highly positive ratio between the utility received and the value given up" (Harrison and Wicks 2013), or greatest value at the lowest cost (Tosti 2001; Bahlis 2006).

The perpetual pull between unique and shared priorities is influenced by a variety of organizational and individual factors. As illustrated in Figure 3-2, these factors include organizational politics, mandates, wants, needs, fear, culture, past experiences, and a variety of cognitive biases, some of which were described in the previous chapter.

Figure 3-2. Factors Influencing Stakeholder Expectations

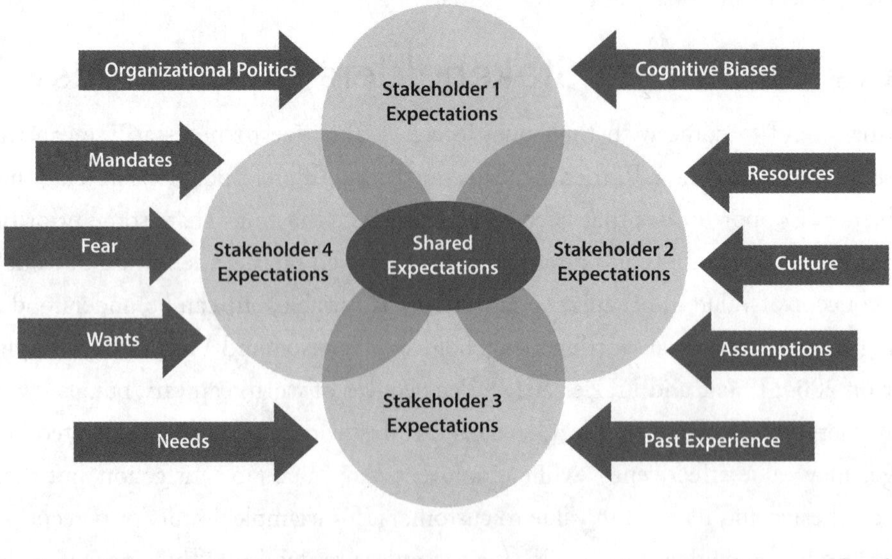

Balancing stakeholder expectations requires assessing, weighing, and addressing the sometimes competing claims of those who have a stake on a specific organizational improvement initiative and the organization's success as a whole. Finding an appropriate balance is important because you—and the organization—don't have the resources to do everything for everyone all the time. As mentioned, the appropriate allocation of resources is a top concern for stakeholders and part of managing an organization is finding a way to "share" rather than "compete" for resources.

Balancing stakeholder expectations can be interpreted as institutional sharing, and sharing is one of the classic signs of prosocial behavior that leads to cooperation and survival of individuals and groups. This cooperation can result in the more efficient deployment of resources in the long run and a reduction in conflict among individuals and groups. You can play a central role in setting up the systems and mechanisms that support a culture of shared expectations and rewards. Therefore, you must apply a thoughtful and effective set of methods to understand the range of expectations that have to be met and how to balance expectations and benefits for the organization and its stakeholders. As a matter of legitimacy and credibility, if you don't regularly meet the expectations of your stakeholder groups, you will lose the confidence and support of the very people you are trying to help.

The rest of this chapter provides you with specific guidance as we follow Kai applying this consultative problem-solving approach by documenting, weighing, and aligning stakeholder expectations.

> While Jessie called Kai to request training, Kai knew Jessie's request for a solution was a signal to help diagnose the problem and find a solution that generated real results. Jessie already signaled an assumption that training was the way to address the teamwork problems and high turnover in the claims department. Using research about the organization, Kai also became familiar with the execution culture that leadership described as focusing on being efficient, effective, and timely. In the first meeting—the discovery meeting—Kai wanted Jessie to describe what the performance currently looked like and share her expectations of what performance should look like after a solution is implemented. During this step, Kai was interested in making connections between performance expectations and organizational priorities.

Scheduling a Discovery Meeting

Setting up a discovery meeting allows you to learn about what prompted the request for help from the L&D team. It is likely your first meeting with the project sponsor and your first opportunity to gain an understanding of the performance issue, its context, and the sponsor's performance expectations.

As discussed in chapter 1, asking the right questions is important in any situation. It is particularly important to begin the strategic alignment process with the right questions, because the answer will influence the direction of your efforts. Some of the overarching questions that guide these types of initial discussions include:

- What evidence of success (tangible result) would you expect to see once this solution is implemented?

- Why is that result important?
- Who else would see the result as important?
- How would that help the organization get closer to its objectives?
- What seems to be driving or sustaining the issue?
- How robust are your sources?
- What other options have you considered or already tried?
- Why this solution rather than other options?
- Why is it important to address these issues now?
- What are some risks associated with these solutions?

It is important to use language that is appropriate to your stakeholders and engage them in a natural dialogue. The discovery meeting is not an interrogation. Different stakeholders will gain different insights from different questions, which will influence their thinking, logic, and way forward. As you continue practicing and gaining experience, you will find the best combination of questions for each stakeholder. As you gain a track record and reputation for helping deliver results, you will also gain more influence and commitment to "getting the facts" before jumping to solutions. This will significantly contribute to reducing wasted time, disgruntled staff, disloyal customers, and other negative results.

Stakeholders may be accustomed to reaching out to the L&D team to request training as their go-to solution without a second thought as to whether it will fix whatever issue they want resolved. A meeting that delves into questions about performance needs may not have been part of the organizational culture in the past. While it may take some adjustment, this is your opportunity to begin changing the paradigm about what products and services your team can offer to support performance in the organization. In time, you and your stakeholders will have a closer consultative relationship focused on strategic decision making that delivers performance results, rather than a strict transactional relationship focused solely on the delivery of a learning service or product, such as a training solution.

To better understand the needs, and what root causes are sustaining them, you must look at organizations as a system. From a system perspective, much of the organizational challenges the requestor is experiencing are driven by circular patterns that are probably invisible. This means that you want to ask questions to help understand the facts, underlying concepts and assumptions, the soundness of the logic of the request, and the desired outcomes, according to the requestor's expectations. Many of these answers will lead you to system issues, and you want to be able to follow up with system-related questions that focus on evidence and relationships between various issues and concerns. You can use questions within a specific focus area to understand the performance problem or opportunity, its context or environment, and performance expectations; then you can begin to make strategic connections to organizational objectives.

Kai reflected on the discovery meeting with Jessie by reviewing the discovery meeting focus areas and sample questions worksheet (Table 3-3). While the meeting was different, and there was uneasiness on both sides, it revealed a good deal of information they would not have uncovered previously. In previous meetings, Jessie would have provided the direction for implementing the solution while Kai had control over the design. Kai left feeling confident that the questions posed were showing a shared accountability for Jessie's results. Jessie and the claims department were not on their own. Neither was Kai. A strategic partnership was developing.

Table 3-3. Discovery Meeting Focus Areas and Sample Questions Worksheet

Questions	Stakeholder Responses
Perceived Performance Challenge or Opportunity	
• What brought the requestor to seek help? • What exactly is being requested (for example, a predetermined solution or help in problem solving)? • How important is this problem or opportunity? • Who is currently being affected and/or whom will it impact? How? • Who may affect it? How? • What evidence has led each stakeholder to his or her conclusions?	• Jessie described poor teamwork and high turnover rates • Jessie requested team-building training on the initial phone call • High importance. Jessie describes the urgency in the claims department: with the recent acquisition of InsCo2, they have close to double the work and new associates learning the job, while at the same time, tenured staff are voluntarily leaving at high rates • A-level agents may affect the project because they have been the most vocal about the "changes in service" InsCo1 and InsCo2 claims associates may impact the adoption of any solution selected. Jessie describes past retreats organized to generate cooperation between the groups. Jessie notes team members need to learn "how to work together cooperatively"
Solution Context and Organizational Environment	
• If a specific solution is being requested, in what ways will the solution be supported in the current work environment? • In what ways may the current work environment impede the solution? • What type of management support (e.g., allocation of resources) exists for the solution(s)?	• Jessie is requesting team building training and has noted several limitations for implementation: • Time away from job • Scheduling all team members to attend in a short timeframe • Past experiences at the team building retreat • The past solution failure may impede solution adoption. Jessie mentioned it can't be "just another fad" • Team members are already feeling stressed and overworked with current workloads and the recent acquisition. The solution must be precise to gain support, credibility, and strategic results. • Jessie has offered support for claims associate time away from the job, but must keep delivery of training (if selected) to two hours or less • The director of operations has agreed to pay overtime, as necessary, for scheduling outside normal work hours

Table 3-3. Discovery Meeting Focus Areas and Sample Questions Worksheet (cont.)

Questions	Stakeholder Responses
Expectations of Performance	
• What does performance look like today? • What results (or outputs) are currently being accomplished? • What should performance look like after the solution is implemented? • What tangible results should be delivered by performers? • What criteria will be used to determine whether these results are satisfactory? • Who will determine or judge whether the results obtained are satisfactory based on these criteria? • What, if any, evidence suggests that employees are clear about the performance expectation? • What if any gaps exist between desired and current results?	• The claims department is currently two weeks behind in their processing schedule (target is to process all requests within three days). Jessie noted an increase in agent complaints about wait times • Each claims associate processes 10 claims forms, on average, per day and interacts with at least five agents per day (target is to process 20 on average per day and 10 agent interactions per day) • Jessie noted, "if we could improve the number of agents claims associates talk to every day and the volume of paperwork processed each day goes up, that will solve my problem." • Jessie, operations manager of the claims department; the director of operations, claims associates, and the agents will determine satisfaction • There is no evidence yet that claims associates are aware of the performance expectations; specifically, how their work was affected by the acquisition of InsCo1 and InsCo2. Claims associates do not have access to a current job description. Performance feedback is provided, formally, once per year.
Connections to Organizational Objectives	
• To what business objective(s) does the performance issue relate? How? • What business goal(s) will our selected solution affect? How and to what extent? • What skills are required to fulfill the performance objective? • In addition to skills, what else (for example, resources and support) may be required to fulfill the performance objective?	• Fully integrating InsCo2 with InsCo1 within two years • Reduce annual voluntary turnover of all operations positions by 7 percent within three years • Improve reputation as a trusted insurance provider • Cooperation, collaboration, strategic skills, system thinking, critical thinking skills • Support will be required from operations management to solve this problem systematically and thoughtfully, before jumping to scheduling or implementing the team building training
Partnership and Collaboration Items	

• What is the best way to collaborate with or support you?
• What other partnerships are critical to the success of our solution(s)?
• How do we ensure these partnerships are effective?
• Describe the process of collaborating with your stakeholders. (What they can expect from you, what you can expect from them throughout the life cycle of the solution?)
• What barriers or challenges might you encounter?
• How can we overcome them?
	• Jessie and Kai agreed to meet face to face once a week for the next four weeks to problem solve and negotiate aligned solutions
	• Invite representatives from the following to the next meeting:
	  ° New and existing claims associates
	  ° Director of operations
	  ° A handful of A-level agents
	  ° Kai's supervisor
	• Approach this meeting similarly to the discovery meeting, as collaborative problem solving, encourage digging deeper before landing on solutions
	• Plan B, if all not comfortable with this approach, offer to conduct as a trial with a smaller group of associates to generate and build support

Kai made sure Jessie knew they were partners in addressing this problem and in finding the solution. Kai sensed Jessie's urgency and how important it was to the claims associates and the agents that the issues with productivity get worked out as quickly as possible. Kai assured Jessie that work would happen quickly and wouldn't take away from the selection of a strategically aligned solution.

The discovery meeting is for establishing a strategic business partnership with the requestor. As you begin to establish this partnership, you also want to verify your notes about who the key stakeholders are and what the requestor sees as their stake and role in these efforts. Consider using the stakeholder mapping tool in the appendix to help guide the discussion about the relative influence and importance of each of these stakeholders.

You will want to define a general approach for engaging these other stakeholders, including whom to contact, when, and how. Defining this stakeholder engagement plan may extend beyond the initial discovery meeting, but the task should be introduced before it concludes as an important next step. This will mark an important start to your partnership with the requestor, as you begin to collaboratively plan how to engage other key individuals and gain their support for proceeding with this important effort. As you continue in this phase, you will also collect information from those individuals to completely understand their wants, perceived issues, challenges, and other relevant information to align the various expectations.

As you embark on the strategic alignment process, you need to ensure you have commitment from the project sponsor in planning, implementing, and sustaining your efforts. If you do not have commitment, you have no tangible connection to the goal or to the strategic alignment efforts. It is important for you and the requestor to clarify the shared and valued goals of the strategic alignment process and approach, as well as anticipate some of the potential obstacles and steps that should be taken to overcome them. This way, you can begin to develop a collaborative relationship that will keep the process moving forward, even in the face of challenges.

Just as with Kai, your approach to addressing the performance problem with the requestor may be slightly different from what you and the requestor are accustomed to. Your prior working relationship with the requestor may not have included an analysis, discussion, and collaborative decision of the appropriate solution. To facilitate this change in the way you do business with the requestor, you want to consider what you can do to facilitate a commitment for change in your problem-solution approach. Here are some general items to consider:

- Develop and foster trusting working relationships.
- Share risks, responsibilities, and rewards.
- Facilitate a culture of cross-functional, interteam collaborative practice.
- Anticipate potential challenges and specific steps to overcome them.

Kai received a good deal of information from Jessie in their discovery meeting. The next step was to understand how others in the organization perceived these issues, and what was important from their perspectives. This would ensure that their perspectives were accounted for and addressed going forward. To successfully improve performance through the chosen initiatives, Kai knew it would be beneficial to ensure that all stakeholders were on the same page regarding the problem and how to address it (although Kai also knew the evidence was insufficient at this point because only Jessie's perspective was accounted for). Any solution selected then was likely to be met with resistance by some, and success could be compromised.

Kai and Jessie brainstormed a list of potential stakeholders by considering who would affect or be affected by their performance improvement decisions. They identified five people:

- Matt—a representative of claims associates that have direct interaction with the work and the primary customer, agents
- Kristen—the director of operations who coordinates work production
- Grace and Dana—representatives of A-level agents who sell and service the company products
- Danielle—the director of talent management and development, overseeing resources for performance improvement initiatives.

With Jessie's agreement, Kai arranged a face-to-face meeting with each person.

Discovering Issues From the Perspectives of Others

You should enlist the help of the requestor to further refine your stakeholder map and define an approach for involving stakeholders appropriately. Assuming you have obtained commitment from the requestor, you will collaboratively develop a plan that defines whom you will contact, when, and how.

This involves developing and fostering a partnership with those who will have the greatest probability to affect or be affected by the L&D decisions. Establishing a partnership with them entails gaining a deeper understanding and appreciation of these stressors and conveying that their contributions are valued and required for the success of your efforts. These stakeholders want to know you are working with them and taking their needs into consideration when finding appropriate solutions to address current organizational needs. This can be a delicate path to walk because stakeholder vantage points can vary, which can influence the apparent priorities. You want to listen to them, and assure them that this information will be considered, without promising that all of their initial requests will be met. Therefore, it is important that you do not make promises you cannot keep, or you risk losing their trust, as well as your credibility and influence to support change within the organization.

For example, when speaking with staff, their perspective may focus on how the change will affect them and what it means to their jobs. Their expectations might have to do primarily with how to improve their circumstances. They may not readily or clearly know the connections between their expectations of performance and support, and the organization's objectives, resources, and policies. As you progress through the various phases of the strategic alignment process, your job will include facilitating awareness of these connections to help them understand organizational realities, which will allow them to begin to manage their own expectations.

Validate Project Request With Others

Checking multiple sources helps you validate the information you have received from the requestor. Using multiple sources to make decisions will reduce possible unintended biases that may come from a single source, and in turn help you bolster your confidence with defining the problem and discussions about potential alternatives. To corroborate the original request, you should compare the responses of others to the same general questions you asked the original requestor in the discovery meeting. The focus now is on gaining an understanding of others' perceptions of performance, specifically:

- What do others perceive as the performance problem or opportunity?
- What are the perceptions of others with regard to the context of the performance problem or opportunity?
- What are others' expectations of performance?
- What do others perceive as the connection between their expectations of performance and the organization's objectives?

Gathering and validating information from others is best conducted through face-to-face methods, particularly in situations in which validating L&D solutions has not been the norm. By meeting face-to-face, you can demonstrate the changing paradigm and bolster your efforts to develop and encourage the support of group decisions regarding performance improvement solution and delivery. Face-to-face is preferred because it gives you greater access to stakeholder information. For instance, being in front of the interviewee is likely to allow you to make stronger connections with stakeholders. It also gives you access to verbal and nonverbal cues, which allows you more flexibility to follow up on critical pieces of information more efficiently and effectively. Face-to-face interviews may give the interviewee a greater sense of trust in anonymity and therefore lead them to open up more.

Phone and Internet-supported interviews can have many of the same benefits as face-to-face, especially if you are using the video conferencing options. They can be more time and cost-effective than face-to-face, but you do lose a bit of that personal connection that can be more easily obtained from physical proximity. However, phone and Internet-supported communication is so ubiquitous today that for many people, it feels quite comfortable and natural.

Email or instant messaging would be best used as methods for following up on additional questions or to confirm information, rather than to hold an entire interview. They provide you with relatively quick responses, are immediately documented, and can be quickly reviewed for reference.

To ensure consistency, you should use the same questions and apply the same techniques (using business language, listening skills, system thinking) that you used in the discovery meeting. Remember that part of the reason you are gathering the perceptions of others is to ultimately align the expectations of multiple stakeholders, so you want to be able to compare the responses of various parties.

> Kai held a face-to-face meeting with those who would be affected by or may affect the problem and the solution. Kai believed that meeting face to face would be conducive to gaining additional insight and move the conversation beyond the more typical discussions of solution design and delivery that is most often conducted through email. Kai used the discovery meeting focus areas and sample questions worksheet to gain various perspectives of desired results, make connections to organizational priorities, and uncover any solutions stakeholders may have in mind at this stage.
>
> Kai learned that new and existing claims associates believe teamwork is not an issue. Matt mentioned how newer claims team members enthusiastically talked about the mentoring and support of seasoned members. Team members from InsCo1 and InsCo2 both expressed getting along well and emphasized concern about the lack of communication on how to integrate their claims processing. Associates commented that little notice was provided about merging the InsCo1 and InsCo2 claims teams, as well as little direction given about how to make that happen while meeting their daily production goals.
>
> A-level agents focused their concerns on the unusually long wait times. While accustomed to two-day turnaround times for their clients, they were now waiting for up to two weeks to hear back from a claims associate. Agents also noted appreciating the ability to speak with specific claims associates, rather than waiting in a general queue to receive timely responses. Kai's supervisor, the director of talent management and development, while supporting Kai's approach, reserved comment to see how key stakeholders would respond.

As in Kai's situation, some of these interviews may lead to new information that you didn't have from the requestor. This presents the opportunity to update your questions, and confirm the information with other stakeholders, and later with the requestor as well. The key is to triangulate sources of information on the important potential issues, challenges, and performance drivers. The better you can triangulate information, the more confidence you can have in the accuracy of the information.

To help you synthesize the information collected, you can use a calibration matrix (Table 3-4). This will allow you to summarize the information into categories and to better illustrate the level of alignment among them.

> Using the responses from the Discovery Meeting Focus Areas and Sample Questions Worksheet, Kai filled out the calibration matrix (Table 3-4). It cataloged what each stakeholder noted as a performance problem or opportunity and the performance context as communicated by that stakeholder. Any connections between the performance problem or opportunity and the organization's strategic objectives were also included.
>
> Kai also reflected on each stakeholder's level of partnership and commitment, and added those to the matrix. Once completed, Kai reflected and considered:
> * Where do stakeholders align to one another? Where do they not?
> * Where do stakeholders align to the business? Where do they not?
> * What is the commitment from all stakeholders to see this initiative through?
> * What are the similarities and differences in stakeholder perceptions of the performance context?
>
> While not everyone perfectly agreed on what the performance challenges were or all the barriers and supports, Kai noticed shared themes among the various perspectives:
> * Everyone agreed the volume of work in the claims department was overwhelming.
> * Everyone agreed the claims department was significantly behind target productivity goals.
> * The claims associates described the problem differently than the manager.
> * There was general agreement about organizational priorities.
> * There was a moderate to high commitment from most stakeholders to address the performance challenges.
>
> Kai now had a good working knowledge of the performance challenges from multiple perspectives of the major stakeholder groups. But Kai was focused on long-term and sustainable solutions, not short-term results. Because work gets done with mutually beneficial relationships, Kai decided to research developing and growing strategic partnerships.

Gain Commitment From Others

Because this approach to building strategic partnerships with your stakeholders may be new to your organization, it is critical that you take the lead in gaining commitment from all stakeholders to ensure the process is adopted and others are engaged. This requires a consultative approach and close collaboration between you and the stakeholders. As such, you are not really "providing" solutions, as much as creating positive change together. A commitment to work together is critical. Some ways to gain this commitment are presented in the following sections.

Table 3-4. Calibration Matrix

Stakeholder	Performance Problem or Opportunity		Performance Context			Alignment to Organizational Objectives	Partnership and Commitment		
	Perceived problem or opportunity	Performance expectations	Culture	Supports	Barriers	Organizational objectives being addressed	Resistance level	Solution openness level	Overall commitment level
Jessie operations manager of claims department	Poor teamwork High turnover	More cooperation among InsCo1 and InsCo2 claims associates	Execution-based "getting it right the first time"	Leadership management	Time away from work Scheduling Work volumes Past solutions not working	Fully integrating InsCo2 with InsCo1 by year 2020 Reduce annual voluntary turnover of all operations positions by 7% by year 2021 Improve reputation as a trusted insurance provider	H M L	H M L	H M L
Danielle, director of talent management	We're losing people at an alarming rate Increased number of employee complaints	Keep employees and develop their careers	Execution-based culture Quick results Increased pressure to use data	Supportive leadership team Open to new ideas Can secure budget easier when data are used	Unable to keep up balancing seasoned associates leaving and ramping up new associates	Raise the employee engagement rates each year Reduce voluntary turnover Maintain our reputation as a trusted insurance provider	H M L	H M L	H M L

							H M L	H M L	H M L
Matt claims associate	Lack of communication from leadership and management Lack of process to integrate work Difficulty meeting daily productivity goals	Increased communication about acquisition (what does this change mean to claims associates? How does each fit in?) Understanding work expectations	Execution-based "getting it right the first time"	Leadership Management	Time away from work Scheduling Work volumes Past solutions not working Lack of documented procedures Always training someone new	Fully integrating InsCo2 with InsCo1 by year 2020 Reduce annual voluntary turnover of all operations positions by 7% by year 2021 Improve reputation as a trusted insurance provider	H M L	H M L	H M L
Grace and Dana A-level agents	Long wait times Loss of key contact in Claims department Responses to inquiries can vary depending on who gives you the answer	Reduced wait times	Describes as "fast paced"	Well-developed relationships between sales department and agents and their respective broker and dealer firms	Work with many insurance carriers	Improve reputation as a trusted insurance provider	H M L	H M L	H M L
Kristen director of operations	Lack of teamwork in the claims department Claims not meeting daily or weekly goals	Reduce wait time for A-level agents Increase claims productivity Claims associates are not aware of changing regulations	Execution-based culture Cooperation	Flexible scheduling options Can leverage other teams as necessary for improvement efforts	Claims volume is predicted to increase over next quarter Risk of not meeting quarterly sales goals	Fully integrating InsCo2 with InsCo1 by year 2020 Reduce annual voluntary turnover by 7% by year 2021 Improve reputation as a trusted insurance provider	H M L	H M L	H M L

Discuss the Collaboration Opportunities

A collaborative approach to your work is essential to shaping the expectations and accountabilities of L&D decisions. This approach also bolsters cross-functional relationship building and improves others' perceptions of you as a strategically valuable business partner. Be clear about their role in these collaboration opportunities, and what specifically can be expected of them, so they understand what they are committing to and can prepare accordingly.

Describe the Strategic Alignment Objectives and Process

Your description of the purpose and value of the strategic alignment approach, as well as what it entails and how others are involved helps your stakeholders understand what to expect from you and what you expect from others. This also communicates how working together to address the performance problem or opportunity is a joint effort with everyone sharing input and accountability.

Negotiate Communication Plans

Your communication plan describes how each stakeholder is engaged in the process. It is important to uncover the stakeholder's point of view in communication; for example, availabilities, access to communication methods, and roles and responsibilities.

Identify Potential Drivers and Barriers

The analysis, design, implementation, and tracking of results will be influenced by both drivers and barriers. Drivers are those factors that help facilitate successful execution of each stage. Barriers are those factors that may impede successful execution of each stage. When identifying potential drivers and barriers, consider the following:

- expectations
- feedback
- tools and resources
- consequences
- incentives
- skills and knowledge
- selection and assignment
- motives
- preferences
- management
- culture and environment.

Aligning Stakeholder Expectations

Now that you have gathered the perspectives of your original requestor and other stakeholders, you need to synthesize these perspectives while maintaining and balancing the best interests of the business and each stakeholder. The following questions will help you interpret the information you collect in your calibration matrix across the various sources:

- Is there consensus among the various stakeholders about the problem or opportunity to be addressed? If not, why?
- Is there consensus about the magnitude of the problem or opportunity?
- Is there consensus about who will be affected by the chosen solution?
- Does everyone share an understanding of the business goal being addressed?
- How consistent are performance expectations?
- How clear are the performance expectations?
- Is there agreement that a skill gap exists?
- If not a skill gap, is there agreement to explore noninstructional solutions?

When synthesizing the perspectives, you will consider and weigh the credibility of the information provided to you. Specifically, you will analyze the relevancy, reliability, validity, and thoroughness of the information:

- **Relevant:** The information provided is directly related to the performance problem or opportunity.
- **Reliable:** The information provided is measurable, trustworthy, and consistent (rule of thumb: three or more sources to corroborate the information).
- **Valid:** The information is based on logic or fact and considers other plausbile factors, causes, or relationships.
- **Thorough:** The information does not omit important elements, as available.

Place a check mark next to each criterion that estimates the credibility of the information you are receiving from each stakeholder. Use the results of this assessment to help you assign appropriate weights to competing information. Table 3-5 gives an example. Your responses may reveal that not everyone has consistent views about the key issues and what results are most important. In addition to using the matrix above for comparing stakeholder perceptions and expectations, you can also use the information you have collected to map your initial understanding of the issues or opportunities.

> To complete the Information Credibility of Stakeholder Expectations template, Kai considered the credibility of the information provided by each of the stakeholders and used it to determine whether additional information should be gathered before making robust conclusions.

Table 3-5. Information Credibility of Stakeholder Expectations

Stakeholder	Performance Expectations			
	Relevant	Reliable	Valid	Thorough
Jessie, operations manager claims department	✔	✔		
Matt, claims associate	✔	✔	✔	✔
Grace and Dana, A-level agents	✔	✔		
Kristen, director of operations	✔	✔		

Mapping Performance Issues Within the System

Chapter 2 introduced four levels of alignment. You now have a wealth of information about how stakeholders see the major problems, barriers, and success drivers. You can begin to depict apparent relationships among the various issues and problems expressed by stakeholders. At what level are the problems most pressingly observed or felt? Are they primarily concerned with knowledge and skill requirements? Are the central issues or opportunities primarily focused on the work outputs and requirements? Do they affect the organization and cut across specific groups of employees, functions, or departments? Are there significant problems or opportunities related to external clients and society?

From a living system perspective, systems are nested and interconnected, where problems, symptoms, and root causes are all interconnected in some way. Likewise, change can be achieved by pushing simultaneously at different levels. Still, stakeholders will have helped you establish some boundaries for your work.

It is important to note, however, that it is doubtful that you can map your organizational system perfectly. Rather, this exercise can help you to conceptualize the change implications and allow a shared understanding to emerge from stakeholder engagement and discussion about the system map. The truth is that many system mapping exercises are inherently limited and should not distract from thoughtful action and ongoing learning. As a result, some system maps are deliberately high-level abstractions that identify the principle components and relationships in a system, but are intended to act as a basis for discussion rather than a complete description of reality; this contrasts with other system maps that are incredibly detailed and attempt to describe the system and its operations.

While we recommend that you complete this exercise on your own to help you synthesize the initial information about stakeholder perceptions, you may want to use this type of mapping activity as a framework for presenting your preliminary findings during your follow-up meeting with the core stakeholder group.

As you map some of the issues onto the levels, consider adding specific information about where stakeholders' perspectives seem to lie, to help anticipate what to expect when you have follow-up meetings to select the alignment level. You can use this information as well as the stakeholder mapping information to understand the perceptions, priorities, and expectations of your stakeholders, and in turn, be more effective in influencing them.

> To complete the alignment map (Figure 3-3), Kai reflected upon each stakeholder response about the perceived issues and thought about where each issue fit within the system. Kai then documented stakeholder responses about the perceived issues at the level where the problem resided. The stakeholders approached their description of the problem where they experienced it day to day.

Figure 3-3. Alignment Mapping

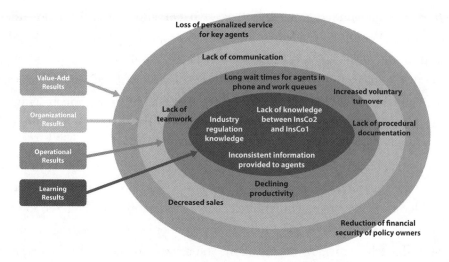

Just as documenting stakeholder responses in the alignment mapping tool facilitated Kai's big-picture view of the problem and opportunities, you now need to decide where the performance issues fall within the system. Use your best judgment here—be cautious about counting the number of occurrences in each level, but rather look for the potential synergy of the parts that are working together to influence performance. The level at which you select to intervene will become your focal point for solution selection later in the process. You will still account for the organization's response at all levels, but start here when thinking through the solutions most closely tied to the problem.

Selecting the Alignment Level

When you are comfortable with the utility and clarity of the completed alignment map and have a good idea of the level of alignment that you would recommend, it's time to facilitate a dialogue about the information you have gathered and where the main issues are with your key stakeholders. You will not necessarily meet with everyone you interviewed, but you will meet with a core group that has clear decision-making authority for your efforts. (The initial requestor should help you identify this group.) You do not have to identify who said what, but share the preliminary information about where issues seem to lie within the organization. The goal is to walk away from this conversation with an agreement about the focus and expected results of the alignment efforts, and their commitment to support the process.

Use the information you have and consider the most appropriate alignment level. It is often very useful to use the preliminary alignment map to present your interpretations and generate discussion among the core stakeholder group. Remember that these levels are part of one organizational system, and in reality the perceived organizational issues or opportunities cut across these levels. When working with clients, we recommend always aligning efforts to value-add results, because that is what organizations exist to do—they exist to meet societal needs. To the extent that your focus and energy is on meeting the ultimate needs of the organization's clients and beneficiaries, you can broaden your view and focus on true strategic priorities, and in turn increase your range of options for how best to get there. The more focused you are on the lower levels of alignment without clearly understanding their relationship to the higher levels of alignment and results, the greater your risk of failure.

We understand, however, that it can be challenging to gain commitment from some of the organizational partners to incorporate alignment of their L&D initiative to strategic value-add level. Use the alignment level selection considerations in Table 3-6 to help clarify the purpose, benefits, risks, and potential impact of either incorporating or ignoring each level. This table provides considerations you can use to help make the decision about how to align your work from this point forward. You can make a selection using the information you gathered from your stakeholders to determine what level the symptoms are present in, and to which level stakeholders have expressed commitment. It will be important to engage your stakeholders to reach agreement on the selected alignment focus—why the approach is the most suitable to the problem, how it may be carried out, and the roles and expectations of your stakeholders going forward.

Discuss how the alignment levels are connected with your stakeholders. For example, if alignment to employee outputs is selected as the primary focus, continue the discussion to establish the connections to specific organizational objectives and priorities, and thus, external value to clients. Your stakeholders may choose to formally exclude some of the higher levels, but it is your responsibility to explain the risks and failure scenarios.

The alignment choice made here will direct your workflow for the remaining steps, so this choice is important; as such it will involve both you and your stakeholders. A follow-up meeting after you have integrated the various stakeholder expectations and map the presenting symptoms according to the various vantage points is an effective way to discuss key issues and agree on the alignment level and way forward.

Kai met with stakeholders to discuss the completed alignment map to determine an appropriate alignment level to begin focusing their efforts. Many felt the work should begin at the level at which each is directly feeling the problem, while others discussed solutions to remedy these problems. Kai maintained a focus on the alignment level (and on defining the problem before landing on any solution).

Kai listened to the feedback from these stakeholders and agreed that the operational level would be a useful place to begin, because that was where this group would have the most immediate influence and could help frame the conversation about alignment to other levels as their work progressed.

Gaining Commitment on Direction, Scope, and Approach

Partnerships with key stakeholders require formal agreements on specific steps to be taken to address shared needs. A clear plan should include who is responsible for doing what and when, as well as how to establish clear accountabilities. As you finalize your efforts in this expectation alignment phase, complete the following tasks with your stakeholders:

- Describe the rationale for alignment to others.
    - Offer support to communicate why alignment is best given the perspectives and criteria as you know them today.
    - Describe the features of the alignment level selected:
        - purpose
        - benefits (anticipated and realized)
        - risks (anticipated and mitigated)
        - costs (anticipated, tangible, intangible)
        - impact potential.
- Describe the process for the selected alignment level.
    - How long do you anticipate it will take to carry out?
    - What project roles and responsibilities will be required to carry out the selected alignment level?
- Negotiate and confirm the communication plan for the process from this point forward.
- Discuss and clarify expectations of success upon successfully completing the strategic alignment process. (Depending on whether you are an internal or external consultant, this can include full implementation and evaluation of the selected L&D initiatives.)
    - specific results
    - preliminary performance indicators (which will be updated in the alignment of results phase).

Table 3-6. Alignment Level Selection Considerations

Level	Purpose	When to Use	Benefits	Costs and Risks	Impact Potential
Alignment to Value-Add Results	To ensure the solution helps the organization meet the needs of external clients, society, or community.	Collaborators describe a desire to connect work to economic and personal security of external clients, public health, safety, environmental impact, quality of life, survival. The organization wants to ensure long-term survival and profitability. The organization is faced with a significant threat, change, or opportunity from its external environment.	The value added extends outside the walls of the organization and affects society and the community. Organizational results aligned to the well-being of external stakeholders. Greatest opportunity for the organization's sustainability.	May be costly in terms of time and money up front. Realized dividends are long term.	Highest level of strategic impact. Can add value to customers and society at large, an in turn positively affect organizational sustainability.
Alignment to Organizational Results	To ensure alignment between your solution and the organization's bottom line.	Collaborators describe a desire to connect work to market share, revenue, sales, profits, and customer satisfaction.	Helpful in ensuring that all organizational efforts are linked to organizational objectives and priorities. Potential to improve the effectiveness and efficiencies of the organization.	May be costly in terms of time and money up front. Realized dividends are long to midterm.	Potential for high level of impact on bottom line. Can improve organizational effectiveness.

Alignment to Operational Results	To align solutions to specific accomplishments of an individual, group, or department.	Collaborators describe specific performance deliverables of an individual, group, or department. There is a change that will affect job outputs or job requirements	Helpful in aligning the right performance solution to tangible work outputs or products	Assumes alignment to strategic objectives, which may not be substantiated.	Can improve operational effectiveness.
Alignment to Learning Results	To align solutions to "how" work is done.	Collaborators describe a desire to improve or introduce how something is done.	Helpful in ensuring that we do things right.	Assumes positive impact on outputs that may or may not occur.	Can improve efficiency.

Align Expectations Checklist

Use this checklist to ensure you have covered all elements necessary for successful alignment of stakeholder expectations.

Element of Alignment	Yes/No	How To
My System Thinking		
I have carefully thought through the context of the performance challenge or opportunity	Y/N	
My Strategic Thinking		
I have performed an objective analysis by investigating: what, when, why, where, and how	Y/N	
My Critical Thinking		
I recognize that a problem (or opportunity) exists	Y/N	
I have developed an orderly approach in which tasks are organized and problems are recognized based on severity and urgency	Y/N	
I have synthesized information from a variety of sources	Y/N	
I have determined the credibility of the information provided by my stakeholders	Y/N	
I asked the right questions of my stakeholders	Y/N	
My Collaboration With Stakeholders		
I have developed an openness to a variety of perspectives	Y/N	
I have encouraged my stakeholders to develop an openness to a variety of perspectives	Y/N	
I have used effective listening skills to better understand the expectations of my stakeholders	Y/N	
I have communicated my support of teamwork and shared accountability for the performance problem or opportunity	Y/N	
I have used business language with my stakeholders to communicate my understanding of the performance problem or opportunity	Y/N	
I have used business language to communicate the value in creating alignment	Y/N	
Is this the right partner/project to try out a new process for responding to talent development and management requests?	Y/N	

ALIGN Results

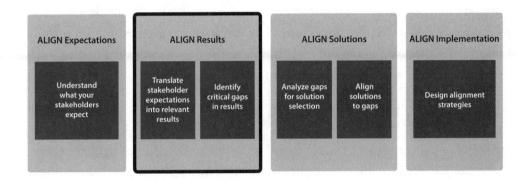

Once you understand what's driving stakeholder decision making (wants, preferences, beliefs, and perceptions), you can determine the measurable organizational results, indicators, independently verifiable data, and critical gaps (needs) you can address. This is the ALIGN Results phase. Table 4-1 shows objectives to accomplish and activities to help you meet them.

Table 4-1. ALIGN Results: Objectives and Activities

Objectives to Accomplish	Activities Designed to Meet the Objectives
• Translate stakeholder wants and expectations into relevant and desired results in learning, operational, organizational, and value-add levels	• Identify relevant results, metrics, and performance targets • Estimate the gaps in results • Compare current performance with desired performance • Assess performance context
• Align L&D work to strategic priorities • Build strategic relationships with stakeholders	• Identify current level of results • Depict relationships between organizational goals, strategic priorities, and stakeholder expectations • Collaboratively design a data collection strategy
• Conduct an ongoing reflection of your work	• Review the ALIGN Results checklist continually to assess your performance

The ALIGN Results phase starts with discovering more information relevant to the key issues identified in the ALIGN Expectations phase. During this phase, you will be aligning client wants and expectations with valued and clearly defined organizational results. You will determine the key results the organization wants to achieve, while avoiding the temptation to commit to what it will take to get there at this point. You will discover more relevant results by examining stated goals and priorities, strategic plans, operational plans, action plans, current or past performance reports (including those from other consultancies or studies), strategic reviews, and any other relevant sources of performance information. You will also work with stakeholders to determine what successful achievement of those goals or worthy performance looks like. Essentially, you will ask: "How will we know when we've successfully reached the goal?" "What are the markers along the way we should pay attention to so we can track our progress toward the goal?" Knowing this information, you can then determine the gaps between the desired level of performance results and the current levels of those results.

Distinguishing Means From Ends

The key to any successful journey is arriving at the right place, at the right time, and in good condition. First, defining the right place is vital. Identifying where you should head and justifying why you should get there will provide you with the critical data on which to design, develop, implement, manage, and evaluate your L&D solutions.

You began to define the direction of the journey in phase 1, when you identified the expectations of stakeholders. As noted, if there is a universal weakness in how organizations go about deciding how to improve their effectiveness and efficiency, it is that they tend to start with solutions rather than a clear understanding of the problem they want to address. While you may have useful information and consensus about some of the key issues that must be addressed from the perspective of stakeholders, the ultimate success of your efforts depends on the extent to which your solutions can contribute to organizational results. Whether you can fulfill this promise depends on you and your team being able to distinguish means from ends (Kaufman 2000).

Reaching our ends is about delivering results. Simply stated, a result is the effect of doing something—it is not what we do, but the consequence it brings. But delivering solutions is not the same as delivering results. We implement solutions to achieve positive results that our organization values.

Means are the way in which we achieve our ends. They are what we do and how we do it. We often have various means from which to choose, but do not always stop to consider the full range of options. The clearer we define our problems in terms of measurable results (and root causes, as we will discuss in the next chapter), the clearer our full range of means becomes. Means are important but there is little inherent value in consuming resources in activities, solutions, and initiatives if they do not help us arrive at a desired end or result. Table 4-2 provides a side-by-side comparison of some examples.

Table 4-2. Means vs. Ends

Ends	Means
Increased sales	• Increased the sales force • Increased knowledge in the sales force in upselling or cross-selling
Reduced the turnover rate of new employees	• Updated benefit package • Launched new employee onboarding program
Reduced defects	• Formed multidisciplinary teams for the product development process • Implemented Six Sigma
Increased customer satisfaction scores	• Reduced turnaround time from order to delivery • Improved communication about how to better use products
Increased profit margin	• Cut low-margin clients, products, and services

Sometimes, the means distract us on our way to the desired results. You may want your team to achieve higher productivity, but if you focus on training them, or transforming them into a "self-directed work team," rather than on foremost reducing the productivity gaps, you risk becoming attached to the means and ignoring evidence that suggests these are not the best means. Recall the discussion of the escalation of commitment or the sunk-cost cognitive trap in decision making, which leads you to throw good money after bad. You decide whether to stay with ineffective means based on what you have already spent on them, rather than on future costs and benefits. The best way to minimize this risk is by remaining flexible about how you reach your ends, and focusing instead on your defined results: where you want to go. It is also important to understand the factors that influence your route to those results, as they give us clues about what routes you will have to take to get there in the most efficient and effective ways.

Objectives

Our definition of results can often be stated in terms of general goals (something we aim for or seek), or in more specific terms that include the precise result of what will be accomplished, a timeline for when it will be accomplished, the conditions under which the result will be observed, and specific targets or measurable criteria to judge the degree to which the result was accomplished. Results stated with this level of precision are called objectives.

But not all objectives are about results. While results-oriented objectives focus on output and outcomes of interest to the organization, process-oriented objectives express the concrete actions to be taken to achieve those outputs and outcomes. An example of a results-oriented objective is, "100 percent of our salespeople will deliver informational product-use presentations by the end of the first year." An example process-oriented objective is, "By the end of Q2 this year, we will launch a new customer information program on how to better use our products."

Looking deeper, not all results are equal. In fact, they exist in networks and hierarchies. For example, there is a distinction between work output objectives, organizational objectives, and value-add objectives. That is, people produce work outputs to contribute to greater organizational objectives, and add value to customers and society:

- **Work Output Objective:**
  - Increase the percentage of salespeople to 100 percent who are delivering informational product-use presentations by the end of Q3 during the first year.
- **Organizational Objective:**
  - Increase sales in North America by 18 percent by the end of the first year.
- **Value-Add Objective:**
  - Decrease injuries due to improper product use to less than two per year by the end of year two.
  - Increase customer satisfaction ratings in North America to a minimum of 96 percent within two years.

It is essential to make a clear distinction between outcome-oriented objectives that reflect the long-term results you want to accomplish; output-oriented objectives that reflect the immediate deliverables of activities, processes, or projects; and process-oriented objectives that reflect how you want to achieve them. For example, launching the new customer information program may be important, but it is important because you want to improve customer satisfaction ratings. Process-oriented objectives can trigger ideas about other comparable alternatives, but only results objectives can help you assess a wider range of appropriate process-oriented objectives.

How do you separate results objectives from process objectives? The most important question is "why?" (or some variation that does not annoy your client while at the same time helps you better understand what they are trying to accomplish). Consider a manager who wants everyone in her sales team to be retrained on proper product usage. Let us say that our L&D specialist simply asked her, "why is that important?" and created a type of cause-and-effect chain with the manager that looks something like this:

Manager: We need to have everyone in our sales team take a refresher training course on proper product usage as soon as possible.

L&D Specialist: Could you help me understand why that is important?

Manager: Because our sales team needs to be able to properly demonstrate to the customer how to use the products.

L&D Specialist: Yes, that certainly makes sense. Can you give me a bit more detail about why the request is being made now?

Manager: Because we have received customer complaints about the products not working well.

L&D Specialist: I see the urgency behind your request. Customer satisfaction is central to our business success. This sounds like it could affect a number of other important business issues and requires our full attention.

Manager: Yes, exactly! Our returns are up and sales are down. And at this point, we can expect to get lower customer satisfaction scores.

L&D Specialist: Count on our support to help. By the way, would you mind if we reviewed those customer complaints to get a better understanding of their specific concerns? There might be some useful information to help us fine-tune our solutions.

Manager: Sure, it sounds as though you understand what we're trying to do here. It would be great to get your input if you see anything important that we may have missed. I'll have the customer reports sent to you as soon as possible.

Notice how the L&D specialist's line of questioning comes from a "Help me understand; I want to help" perspective that enables them both to make the connection between the request for training and the business needs. In this case, the L&D specialist used this opportunity to request further information that might help solve the problem by fine-tuning the solution. With additional documented data, the L&D specialist will be better positioned to potentially come back to the manager with reasonably compelling information that would warrant a bit more energy in better defining the problem, and putting the predetermined solution on hold.

Needs

Distinguishing means from ends can be challenging due to our overuse of the word *need*. Just listen to everyday conversation. Common use of need often suggests a solution—you need more money, you need more time, you need more people, you need to outsource, you need to reorganize—and this always leads to selecting and applying the solution (more money, more time, and so on) before you know what results should be delivered. Thus, by overusing need, people unthinkingly or unknowingly jump into solutions before defining and justifying the problem they want to solve.

Roger Kaufman, often referred to as the father of needs assessment in the performance improvement field, defines needs as a gap between the results you want and the current results you are accomplishing. He further defines the tool or process for identifying needs a needs assessment. A needs assessment may reveal a number of gaps, and the gaps that are pursued for resolution are what he refers to as the problems we want to solve.

In his view, many so-called needs assessments are not needs assessments, but rather a survey of wants. For example, picking training as a solution, and then asking your employees to come up with five areas in which they think they need training and how they prefer the training to be delivered is not a needs assessment. Rather, this would be an example of how to justify preferred or familiar solutions through incomplete data without first collecting evidence about real work output gaps, actual contributing factors, and a range of relevant options that may be more effective and consume fewer resources.

This chapter identifies gaps in relevant results similar to that proposed by Kaufman. You will learn how to identify relevant results and targets, identify the current level of results, and estimate gaps between desired and current results. Figure 4-1 illustrates the three key steps in this phase.

Figure 4-1. Steps for Aligning Results

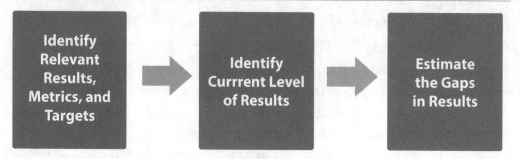

Identifying Relevant Results

In the first phase, your stakeholders provided you with their expectations of success, or what success should look like. With this information, you have the knowledge to successfully meet your stakeholders' perceptions of success. Now, you can identify the measurable indicators (or metrics) of success, or what marker will tell you that you are making progress toward your goals or objectives for the chosen level of alignment.

Value-Add Results

This level is focused on identifying and resolving results gaps between the desired and actual accomplishments of an organization, as measured by the usefulness and value of those accomplishments to the organization's external clients and society (Kaufman 1998, 2000). Relevant results at this level may relate to security, public health, safety, environmental impact, quality of life, and survival of customers, staff, and communities affected by the organization in their course of business.

While these results may seem far removed from the work of employees, the work of employees has the most influence at this level. The work processes, protocols, training, feedback, and supervision have a direct affect on what customers ultimately receive in the way of products and services. Consumers now have the ability to influence a brand's reputation (positively or negatively) with one comment shared on social media for dozens, hundreds, or thousands of people in their networks to see. With globalization and the Internet, consumers have unlimited choices, so the key dimension of differentiation has become the customer experience. When customers are asked how organizations can better engage with consumers to create loyalty and continue to earn their business, well more than half of those asked indicate that improving the overall customer experience is critical. A study of consumers conducted by Oracle (2011) found:

- 86 percent will pay more for a better customer experience
- 79 percent who shared complaints about poor customer experience online had their complaints ignored
- 89 percent began doing business with a competitor following a poor customer experience.

Improving the customer experience to achieve high levels of customer satisfaction can directly influence organizational performance measures, such as an increase in sales, loyal customers, and referrals. Yet, while critical to success, this value-add level of results is not usually addressed by L&D solutions.

This level embodies system thinking perhaps better than the other levels. While it is relevant for moving you toward a more proactive approach to organizational change and long-term sustainability, it is particularly important when the organization is engaged in a strategic planning process or faced with a significant organizational change, threat, or opportunity from the external environment.

Results at this level can be found as strategic aims in the form of the organizational vision and strategic objectives. Consequently, strategic plans are a primary source of information in determining concrete results to be delivered at this level. Strategic implementation plans, if available, are another great source of information because they provide more detail on the various organizational actions related to supporting specific strategic objectives. However, it should be noted that not all organizations follow through on their strategic plan with a clear implementation plan. Also helpful are strategic measurement frameworks. For example, if your organization is using a strategic planning and management system, such as the Balanced Score Card (Kaplan and Norton 2004), there should be—in theory—clear results and metrics related to customer satisfaction and impact. The Balanced Scorecard was originated by Robert Kaplan (Harvard Business School) and David Norton as a performance measurement framework that added strategic nonfinancial performance measures to traditional financial metrics to give managers and executives a more "balanced" view of organizational performance.

Organizational Results

This level is focused on identifying and resolving results gaps between the desired and actual accomplishments of the typical organization's bottom line, regardless of the value it may provide to external clients and society. Relevant results at this level may relate to market share, revenue, sales, profits, and customer satisfaction. Customer satisfaction could actually appear both here at the organizational level and the value-add results level, depending on the indicators used to measure it. At the value-add results level, the focus is on long-term satisfaction trends because it indicates a continuous focus and satisfaction on customer needs. On the other hand, this organizational level may focus on one point in time, rather than a trend.

For a healthcare system, organizational results might be patients successfully discharged, expense per episode of care, shared savings, or financial gains or risks from performance-based contracts. For an educational organization, it might be graduation rates, performance on national and state standardized tests, enrollment rates, retention rates, or perhaps secured funding, if it is tied to performance.

This level of result will help you ensure that your L&D solutions contribute to the bottom line, at least in the short run, because there may not be a clear relationship to long-term sustainability, which is most closely related to the value-add results described previously.

Here too, the strategic plan, implementation plan, annual action plans, and strategic measurement frameworks and systems will provide a wealth of information. Mission statements often include the specific accomplishments an organization commits to achieve, although some do not use specific or measurable terms. In this case, your task is to translate "being the best" or "trying hard" into measurable results. Therefore, you must also consult any internal reports that show valued results, based on what is measured to track the organization's progress toward bottom-line targets. These may include annual and quarterly reports that are presented to senior leadership to give them an overview of the organization's performance.

Operational Results

This level is focused on identifying and resolving results gaps at the individual, group, or functional performance level. Essentially, these results are the building-block objectives that when taken together help the organization reach its bottom-line objectives and add value to its customers and society.

Relevant accomplishments at this level tend to relate to specific performer deliverables: successfully completed service call, successfully repaired automobile, sales transaction executed. For a healthcare organization, this might include registrations or admissions errors, average length of stay, maintained bed occupancy, and other operational effectiveness and efficiency measures. For an educational institution, this might include mastery of specific subject areas, successful course completion, instructor effectiveness, and student attendance.

It is important to note that there may be various layers of operational results that work together to deliver a higher level of organizational results. Be sure to carefully identify these value chains so that you understand relevant relationships and interactions.

Likewise, you should carefully consider the alignment of performance results at this level to the two higher-order results discussed previously. Even if you did not gain consensus from stakeholders to estimate gaps in results at the value-add or organizational level, you still want to, at a minimum, confirm strategic connections of performance gaps to strategic objectives.

For example, your key stakeholders may have asked you to focus on resolving employee performance issues that are affecting the error rate in the southeastern plant, but that you do not have to collect data on how these errors affect customers or how these defects affect the community where the plant is located. In this case, at the very least, you want to establish or map out the connection between the errors and broader organizational objectives as it relates to quality, customer satisfaction, and market share objectives. You may not spend much time measuring specific gaps between specific quality, customer satisfaction, and market share targets and "actuals," but at least make clear the strategic value of reducing those error rates and staying solution neutral until you have the facts. Whatever solutions you come up with later will also have to conform to quality standards, policies, and protocols of the organization.

The primary sources of information for establishing relevant performance results include job descriptions, performance plans and evaluations, and performance management frameworks, documentation, and systems.

Learning Level

The learning level focuses specifically on knowledge, skills, and behaviors. While these three terms are often used interchangeably, they are different and should be clearly defined before they can be measured. Knowledge is the theoretical or practical understanding of a particular topic or subject. Possessing an understanding of a concept does not mean the individual knows how to apply the concept. You may have an understanding of the Balanced Scorecard, but it doesn't mean you can, or have ever, used it. The transfer or application of that knowledge is the actual skill. Skill development requires practice, not necessarily more knowledge. Skills define specific learned activities, which can range widely in terms of complexity. Knowing which skills an employee possesses can help you determine whether their training and experience is appropriate for the work activities required for the job. In turn, the specific ways in which one can apply a skill can vary depending on specific behaviors. In other words, differences in skill level might be observed through specific behaviors. What specific behaviors does the individual apply to achieve desired results?

The distinction between knowledge, skills, and behaviors and performance can be vague because performance is commonly described as consisting of employee outputs and activities. It's important to make a clear distinction between employee work outputs (what we describe in the operational level) and employee activities. Activities are how people go about producing work outputs, which requires relevant knowledge, skills, and behaviors.

It is also important to highlight the distinctions between what people know and what they can do, because this helps you keep your estimation of learning gaps anchored to specific, clear, and measurable skills and behaviors required to perform the job. Research indicates that training and other knowledge solutions that are focused on relevant work tasks are more successfully transferred to the job than training that is based exclusively on thematic areas or topics (Burke and Hutchins 2008). This distinction helps us begin to design transferability of both knowledge learned and skills practiced in training because it provides the basis for specific behavioral objectives, strategies, activities, and content that are aligned to help the employee successfully perform on-the-job tasks. It also provides the foundation for detailed, corrective, and timely feedback for employees on the job. As research tells us, it is corrections to the specific ways in which work activities get done that produce changes in the work outputs (Kluger and DeNisi 1996). Work output data does not always tell us where the process went wrong and how to correct it. So, we must also look at how people produce or deliver work outputs.

Performance criteria, organizational and industry quality standards, operational procedures and policies, and other organizational policies, norms, regulations, and rules can be useful sources of information for determining what people should be doing to deliver expected results. Job description formats vary, but most may not offer a sufficient level of detail, making it necessary to check various sources.

> Kai consulted the corporate website to learn more about the organization's goals and strategic priorities. Kai also enlisted the support of Kristen, director of operations, for assistance with identifying strategic plans; that of the organization and for the operations division. Kai noticed connections between the overarching goals of the organization and that of the operations strategic plan. Kai then organized the desired results at various levels of the claims project and how those may be connected to the desired goals and strategic priorities of the organization using a logic model design (Figure 4-2).

Figure 4-2. Logic Model

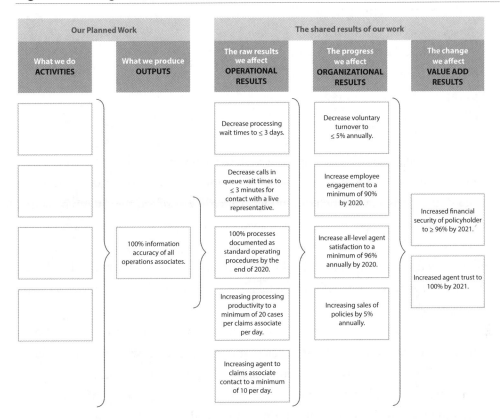

By using a logic model design, Kai was able to depict the relationships between the organization's goals, strategic priorities, and the expectations expressed by stakeholders up to this point. When reflecting on these relationships, Kai paid particular attention to the strategic priority noted by several stakeholders in prior meetings: that of fully integrating InsCo2 with InsCo1. Kai wondered if that was a means, rather than an end.

What would the results of full integration look like? Kai remembered the input from the director of talent management about engagement and made a note to confirm the team's shared understanding that full integration of the people among the insurance companies reflects the organization's priority of a highly engaged workforce. With this map in place, Kai then set out to derive metrics for each of the results depicted in the logic model and to confirm desired results.

Metrics

Not all results are directly and easily observable or measurable. Sometimes you must identify metrics: the specific and observable variables that when tracked systematically over time indicate progress (or lack thereof) toward an objective (Guerra-López 2015; Guerra-López and Norris-Thomas 2011). Metrics be used to measure the:

- presence of something
- degree of something
- type of access to something
- level of use
- extent of an occurrence of something
- relevance of something
- quality of something
- effort required to achieve something.

The metrics you select must be directly related to what's being indicated, and you may need more than one metric to measure something. For example, customer satisfaction can be measured in various ways; depending on what metric you select, the data may paint a different picture. One of the most common metrics for measuring customer satisfaction is customer satisfaction scores obtained through customer surveys. Yet what these surveys tell you can vary from what they actually do. Your company may have fairly good customer service scores, yet your customer referrals could be relatively low, your product returns high, and repeat business low.

This is not to suggest that you have to collect and compare data on every single metric of an objective. There are cost-benefit considerations to selecting which metrics will be used as the basis for your data. What's important is that the metrics you use to measure results can affect your understanding of the facts and your interpretation of reality. This, in turn, can influence the solutions that are recommended.

Many performance indicator frameworks have been proposed over the last decades, including Kaplan and Norton's Balanced Scorecard (2004); Lynch and Cross's Performance Pyramid (1991); the results and determinants framework proposed by Fitzgerald, Johnston, Brignall and Sivestro (1991); and Neely, Adams, and Kennerly's Performance Prism (2002). Your organization may use any or none of these. Your task is to identify the results and metrics that are particularly relevant to the performance issues you are attempting to address, and determine which would best evaluate the effectiveness of your solutions. Table 4-3 offers some examples of metrics you can use.

With a preliminary list of results and metrics for the chosen alignment levels, you are ready to share with the stakeholder group to gain agreement about their relevant and strategic alignment value. This can be either in a formal or casual meeting, depending on what is appropriate in your context. In either case, it should not come as a complete surprise to the stakeholder groups, because you should be keeping in close contact and collaborating as you continue through each step and stage of the strategic alignment process.

Table 4-3. Sample Metrics

Level	Required Results	Sample Metric
External Value-Add	Increased quality of life of customers	• Disabling accidents caused by our product • Deaths attributed to the product • Public image
	Contribute to the health of the served communities	• Toxic pollution reports (compliance certification and/or violations) • Economic contribution to community
Organizational	Increased profit*	• Money collected • Money paid out • Total assets
	Increased customer satisfaction*	• Customer satisfaction scores • Customer loyalty • Customer complaints • Average duration of active accounts • Number of products sold per account
	Employee satisfaction	• Employee satisfaction scores • Filed grievances • Documented complaints • Performance levels • Turnover rates • Absenteeism
Operational	Sales*	• Items sold (service or product) • New accounts generated • Inventory turnover • Sales volume • Sales per channel • Frequency (number of sales transactions)
	Increased Quality Production	• Production rate • Error rate • Efficiency • Rework • Rejects

*Sales could be seen as an organizational or performance result, depending on whether you are viewing the organizational aggregate sales or specific individuals or sales teams.

Kai met with the team to discuss the relationships between the organization's goals and strategic priorities, as well as the expectations communicated by each stakeholder, which are now expressed as desired results (Figure 4-3). The team was interested in looking at the map closer to learn more about the relationships, and they began discussing potential chain reactions and how each level of result may influence another. Kai was onto something here, and moved to secure commitment to finding evidence for each specified result. Kai emphasized that everyone knows where they want the organization to be, and how interesting it would be to see where the results currently are. Kai then led the group through a discussion about what evidence would show how the company was performing in each area. Kai documented the team's decisions, noting them as indicators to inform each result.

Figure 4-3. Alignment of Indicators to Results

Our Planned Work		The shared results of our work		
What we do **ACTIVITIES**	What we produce **OUTPUTS**	The raw results we affect **OPERATIONAL RESULTS**	The progress we affect **ORGANIZATIONAL RESULTS**	The change we affect **VALUE ADD RESULTS**

Operational Results:
- Decrease processing wait times to ≤ 3 days. — *Days to process*
- Decrease calls in queue wait times to ≤ 3 minutes for contact with a live representative. — *Queue wait time in minutes*
- 100% processes documented as standard operating procedures by the end of 2020. — *# standard operating procedures*
- Increasing processing productivity to a minimum of 20 cases per claims associate per day. — *# of cases processed*
- Increasing agent to claims associate contact to a minimum of 10 per day. — *# of agent/ to claims associate interactions*

Outputs:
- 100% information accuracy of all operations associates. — *Quality Assurance Score*

Organizational Results:
- Decrease voluntary turnover to ≤ 5% annually. — *Voluntary turnover rate*
- Increase employee engagement to a minimum of 90% by 2020. — *Employee engagement score*
- Increase all-level agent satisfaction to a minimum of 96% annually by 2020. — *Satisfaction rating*
- Increasing sales of policies by 5% annually. — *# of sales*

Value Add Results:
- Increased financial security of policyholder to ≥ 96% by 2021. — *Policyholder Feedback Score*
- Increased agent trust to 100% by 2021. — *Agent Feedback Score*

Targets

With a firm agreement on the results of interest, you want to also ensure you have targets for each metric. Targets are specific planned levels of accomplishment for a specific metric within a specific timeframe. Targets motivate people to achieve because they give them something concrete to pursue. They also help you interpret progress as either at, below, or above expectations, with "expectations" in this sense representing the specific target. Therefore, they help us detect gaps and trigger corrective action.

For example, if the objective was to increase the sales closing ratio of the northeast sales team to 30 percent by the end of this year, your indicator is "sales closing ratio" and your target is 30 percent. When you collect data about the current closing ratio of the sales team and find that their closing ratio as a group is actually 17 percent, you are able to interpret that this is a gap, which signals that an analysis of this gap is warranted to understand why the gap exists, and in turn take the appropriate corrective actions.

You may find targets in the documents you review and in the management information systems the organization uses. Many organizations use automated scorecards or dashboards that electronically track relevant organizational data and offer gauges to signal the extent to which current performance levels meet target numbers. In other cases, those targets may not be clear yet, and you and your stakeholders will want to work together to set appropriate targets based on past performance, performance from top performers, industry standards, or expert judgment. The point is that you must have specified targets against which to compare and interpret the actual level of performance.

Discovering the Current Level of Results

In the previous step you spent time looking through organizational records, reports, and systems, as well as communicating and confirming with your stakeholders what measures of success should be used to direct and demonstrate valued results. At the same time, you should have been looking for specific targets that indicated the level of expected accomplishment for that objective. This is the ideal or "what should be" side of the equation.

In this step, you collect data about the current level of performance. Document reviews—records, information systems, reports, and many of the other secondary sources you used in the previous step—are a common method for identifying the current levels of accomplishment for a given indicator.

Other data may not be available, so you will have to collect it. For example, you have already identified through sales reports that there is a substantial gap in the closing sales ratio. Now you want to identify whether there is a gap between the organization's sales process and what the northeast sales team is actually doing. Observation may be the most appropriate way to determine this. You might even set up two different groups to observe. One could include salespeople who have closing ratios that are meeting targets; and the other group would be composed of individuals who are consistently missing their ratio targets. Here, you would be observing the sales process they use, and how it compares to steps from the organization's process, for which they received extensive training and practice prior to going into the field. You may also want to observe what other differences exist between the two groups that might explain the gaps in performance. (The next chapter will explore the process for identifying root causes of performance gaps in more detail. The point to note here is that you will not always find the data about current levels of accomplishments neatly listed on a report or computer screen.)

There are many options for collecting data about current level of performance, including surveys, focus groups, knowledge tests, and various others. Here are some of the considerations to keep in mind when planning data collection:

Consider the type of data you are seeking, and whether the methods and tools you are considering are appropriate for those types of data. For example, if you are looking for a sales team's sales volume, you would not want to conduct a survey or focus group to find out what people "think" the sales volume is. You would want to go directly to organizational records. Conversely, if you are looking to measure the satisfaction of the sales team with the sales incentive package, you probably won't find it in organizational records; you would want to ask the sales team directly how satisfied they are.

There are a number of ways of collecting data about people's perceptions, attitudes, and opinions, including surveys, questionnaires, and interviews. Choosing them in part depends on the size of your group, how dispersed they are geographically, the resources you have available (including time and money), and even whether you or someone in the L&D team has the expertise to design and deploy those methods.

After deciding which indicators would be used to inform results, Kai initiated discussions that focused on the administration of the data collection process; for example, who or where the team would get these data from, how they would go about getting these data, and how the data would be analyzed. Kai recorded the team's decisions in Figure 4-4.

Figure 4-4. Data Collection Strategy

Results		Data Collection			
		Indicators	Sources	Methods	Data Analysis
Stakeholder and organizational desires		Data required to inform progress	Whom and where data are from	How and how often data are collected	How, when, and how often data will be analyzed
Value-Add Results	Increase policy owner financial security to >96% by 2021	Policy owner feedback score	Chief of administration	Annual review of Policy Owner Feedback Report (PFR) generated by web dev team	Agree/Disagree; web dev team each Dec.
	Increase agent trust to 100% by 2021	Agent feedback score	Chief of administration	Annual review of PFR generated by web dev team	Agree/Disagree; web dev team each Dec.
Organiza-tional Results	Decrease voluntary turnover to <5% annually	Voluntary turnover rate	HR performance management system	Quarterly review of HR report	FTE headcount/voluntary; director of TM each Mar.
	Increase employee engagement to 90% by 2020	Employee engagement score	InsCo1 and InsCo2 employees	Annual employee engagement questionnaire	Disaggregate average employee score by division & department; director of TM generates each Mar
	Increase agent satisfaction to 96% annually by 2020	Agent satisfaction rating	Chief of administration	Annual review of agent satisfaction report generated by web dev team	Satisfied/dissatisfied; web dev team analyzes each Dec
	Increase sales of policies by 5% annually	Number of sales	Sales manager	Monthly review of sales report	Target #/current #; sales manager generates
Operational Results	Decrease processing wait times to < 3 days	Days to process	Internal processing software reports	Daily document review of these operations reports for the claims department	Target #/current #; claims manager analyzes daily reports
	Decrease wait times to < 3 min for a live representative	Queue time in minutes	Call center reports		
	100% processes documented as standard operating procedures by end of the year 2019	# of standard operating procedures	Internal processing software reports		
	Increase processing productivity to a minimum of 20 cases per claims associate per day	# of cases per day	Internal processing software reports		
	Increase agent to claims associate contacts to a minimum of 10 per day	# of agent and claims associate interactions per day	Call center reports		
Learning Results	100% information accuracy of all operations associates	Quality assurance score	Quality analyst (QA) report	Monthly review of QA reports	Target avg. %/current avg. %; report is analyzed by senior QA to identify patterns in errors

Estimating Gaps in Results in the Chosen Alignment Level

Once you have chosen specific targets for each of your indicators, and gathered the data about the current level of performance, you want to define gaps between the two in a clear and concise way. This is a critical step because you want to have a precise number that helps all involved understand the specific distance to be traveled between where they are now and where they want or should be. For example, if your sales team's closing ratio target is 40 percent, and they are actually closing 25 percent, they are off target by 15 percentage points. Because you need to close this 15-point gap, the overarching objective of the solution you select is to help the team increase their closing ratio by a minimum of 15 percentage points.

In the next phase, when you conduct a causal analysis, you will be able to pair potential solutions to specific causal factors. Notice the difference between this approach to identifying needs and a request from a client that begins with "I need. . . ." What they really mean to say is "I want" or "I think I want." There will likely be more than one solution required, in part because an organizations is a system, and as discussed throughout this book, there are multiple interactions and recurring patterns that reinforce one another to drive the problems we are in the process of defining.

You may find it helpful to illustrate this comparison in a gap chart, similar to the example shown in Table 4-4.

Table 4-4. Illustration of Results Gap Table

	Targets	Actual	Need
Alignment to Value-Add Results	• 0 accidents • 0 loss of life • 0 customer grievances	• 10 accidents per year • 1 loss of life annually • 8 grievances per year	• 10 accidents per year • 1 loss of life • 8 customer grievances
Alignment to Business Results	• Minimum 40% market share • Minimum 35% net profit margin	• 30% market share • 23% in net profit margin	• 10% market share • 12% profit margin
Alignment to Operational Results	• Sales and service acquire at least 20 new accounts per quarter	• 10 new accounts acquired per quarter	• 10 new accounts per quarter
Alignment to Learning	• 100% of customer service agents follow the call escalation protocol • Training is accessible to all employees	• 67% of customer service agents follow the call escalation protocol • 98% of employees can access required training	• 33% of customer service agents do not apply protocol • 2% of employees are without access to required training

Keep in mind that the level of alignment you agreed to ensure with your stakeholders in the previous phase will influence the scope of work for this phase, and you may not have data for all four levels. Your scope may have been for the learning and performance levels, but perhaps did not gain consensus to assess result gaps at the organizational or value-add levels. To strategically align your solutions, you want to link all the way up to organizational results and value-add. Otherwise, you may gain operational alignment, but cannot be certain you have strategic alignment.

> Kai compiled the data from each of the identified sources, and then collaborated with a few stakeholders in analyzing the data to determine and document the gaps—the difference between where InsCo1 is today and where it would like to be. Kai forwarded copies of the Results and Gaps table (Figure 4-5) to each stakeholder for review and to prepare for their next meeting to discuss these gaps.

Figure 4-5. Results and Gaps

Results		Units of Measurement			
		Indicators	Target	Current	Gap
	Stakeholder and organizational desires	Data required to inform progress	Where we'd like to be	Where we are today	The difference between target and current
Value-Add Results	Increase policy owner financial security to > 96% by 2021	Policy owner feedback score	96%	94%	-2%
	Increase agent trust to 100% by 2021	Agent feedback score	100%	93.5%	-6.5%
Organizational Results	Decrease voluntary turnover to < 5% annually	Voluntary turnover rate	< 5% annually	12%	-7%
	Increase employee engagement to 90% by 2020	Employee engagement score	> 96%	94%	-2%
	Increase agent satisfaction to 96% annually by 2020	Agent satisfaction rating	>96%	Level A: 92% Level B: 91% Level C: 94%	Level A: -4% Level B: -5% Level C: -2%
	Increase sales of policies by 5% annually	# of sales	5,250	5,000	-250
Operational Results	Decrease processing wait times to < 3 days	Days to process	< 3 days	10 days	7 days
	Decrease wait times to < 3 min for a live representative	Queue time in minutes	< 3 min	18 min	15 minutes
	100% processes documented as standard operating procedures by end of the year 2019	# of standard operating procedures	58%	100%	42%
	Increase processing productivity to a minimum of 20 cases per claims associate per day	# of cases per day	20 per day	10 per day	10 per day
	Increase agent to claims associate contacts to a minimum of 10 per day	# of agent and claims associate interactions per day	10 per day	5 per day	5 per day
Learning Results	100% information accuracy of all operations associates	Quality assurance score	100%	72%	28%

With a clear list of business needs, you are now ready to begin the process of aligning solutions. The bridge between needs (or problems) and solutions is causal analysis. The prescription should treat the root causes, not just the symptoms.

Align Results Checklist

Use this checklist to ensure you have covered all elements necessary for successful demonstration of aligning results.

Element of Alignment	Yes/No	How To
My Strategic Thinking		
I identified gaps between where the organization is today and where it wants to be in the future	Y/N	
I have assessed the performance context	Y/N	
My Critical Thinking		
I have identified gaps between where the organization is today and where we want to be in the future	Y/N	
I synthesized information from a variety of sources	Y/N	
I determined the credibility of the information I gathered from all relevant sources	Y/N	
I have carefully synthesized the data to identify the appropriate alignment level	Y/N	
I used existing information where possible to avoid duplication when I collected data	Y/N	
My Collaboration With Stakeholders		
I presented coherent and persuasive arguments for controversial or difficult issues	Y/N	
I used my effective listening skills to better understand value from the perspectives of my stakeholders	Y/N	
I collaborated with stakeholders to identify the critical success criteria and measurable indicators for performance improvements	Y/N	
I drove teamwork by recognizing and rewarding the achievement of goals, rather than individual performance	Y/N	
I established partnerships and reduced silo work by teaming up with other groups in the organization	Y/N	
I supported and committed to group decisions that fostered teamwork and shared accountability for our efforts	Y/N	

5

ALIGN Solutions

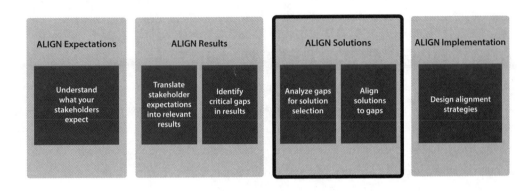

Talent development and other performance improvement solutions can be expensive endeavors for organizations as far as the time, money, and effort required to develop and deliver them. But when properly aligned to performance outcomes, these solutions are no longer seen as "throwaway work." Instead, they become strategically valuable—to both the organization and the employees for whom they're designed.

Throughout the ALIGN Solutions phase, you're striving to make strategically aligned and collaborative decisions about the performance gaps you need to address and how you will address them. Your aim is to find the best investment solutions—ones with timely implementation, with the greatest chance of being adopted by employees, and with the highest return on investment. Table 5-1 lists objectives to accomplish and activities to help you meet them.

Table 5-1. ALIGN Solutions: Objectives and Activities

Objectives to Accomplish	Activities Designed to Meet the Objectives
• Analyze and align gaps in performance • Determine alignment level of performance gaps	• Align performance gaps to level of results • Collaboratively identify gaps to address
• Identify root causes of gaps in performance results	• Conduct root causes analysis • Identify barriers and supports to successful solution implementation

Table 5-1. ALIGN Solutions: Objectives and Activities (cont.)

Objectives to Accomplish	Activities Designed to Meet the Objectives
• Analyze and select solutions aligned to gaps in performance	• Identify shared solution selection criteria • Facilitate aligned solution selection decision making • Define critical factors that will facilitate successful and sustainable implementation of the solutions • Select aligned solutions
• Conduct an ongoing reflection of your work	• Ongoing review of the ALIGN Solutions checklist to assess your performance

Analyzing Performance Gaps

In the last step of ALIGN Results, you charted a comparison between current performance and desired performance. This comparison led to specific and measurable gaps in performance results (-10 accidents per year, -10 percent market share, -10 new accounts per quarter). Using these gaps as evidence, you can now engage your stakeholders in a discussion about which gaps to close and which gaps to ignore or postpone.

Using the information from the last phase, Kai identified gaps within each level of alignment:
- Value-Add
    - -2% policy owner security feedback score
    - -6.5% agent feedback score
- Organizational
    - -7% voluntary turnover rate
    - -2% employee engagement score
    - -4% (A), -5% (B), -2% (C) agent satisfaction rating
    - -250 in number of sales
- Operational
    - +7 days wait time for processing
    - +15 minutes time in queue
    - -42% documentation of standard operating procedures
    - -10 cases per day
    - -5 agent to claims associate interactions per day
- Learning
    - -28% information accuracy

The next meeting with the project team was used to review the gaps in performance results. When reviewing the evidence, Kai described the performance gaps in specific and measurable terms. The team noticed how none of the performance gaps described needing something, such as when Jessie first reached out to Kai with a need for team-building training to solve the problems in the claims department. Investigating true gaps in performance helped the team discover what the problems were. And with that evidence to support decisions about which solutions to choose, Kai led the team to strategic decisions, created strategic alignment between L&D work and the business, and deepened strategic relationships with stakeholders.

Using Kai's example, these gaps influence results at all four levels: value-add, organizational, operational, and learning. However, you cannot realistically address all of these gaps in performance at one time, so it is helpful to determine the criteria you and your stakeholders will apply to handle gaps in performance. Which gaps should you tackle first? Second? Should you tackle a few at once?

To better understand which gaps to address, it is important for you and your stakeholders to negotiate and decide the criteria that will be most important, given the context and realities of the business, so that everyone is on the same page about how to make selection decisions before making them. Some criteria that may be important for your stakeholder to consider include:

- How high of a priority is it to close the gap?
- What employees, departments, and customers are affected by the gap?
- What is the estimated scope of the work, as well as the financial and nonfinancial costs involved in closing the gap?
- How important is closing the gap to management? To employees? To clients?
- What are the anticipated financial and nonfinancial consequences and risks of not closing the gap?
- What is the magnitude of the gap?
- What are the potential consequences to higher alignment levels?

Kai's team reviewed the list of identified gaps, and the conversation quickly moved to negotiating the most important ones to the stakeholder. Kai then asked each stakeholder to complete the gap selection criteria rubric (Table 5-2) individually by rating how important each criterion was to making a decision about solutions. By collaboratively identifying these criteria, Kai was able to continue creating strategic relationships with stakeholders, developing a deeper understanding of what criteria they use to make decisions, and learning how to successfully meet stakeholder expectations.

Kai tallied the responses from each stakeholder to determine which criteria should would be given the greatest consideration when making decisions about which gaps to address and when (Table 5-3).

Table 5-2. Gap Selection Criteria Rubric

Gap Selection Criteria	Description and Considerations	Stakeholder Rating (3 = High; 1 = Low)		
		Jessie	Matt	Kristen
Priority	• High—Must address now • Medium—May address in near future, add to a future phase, or postpone • Low—Can ignore	3	3	3
Scope involved in closing the gap	• Activities and tasks required to do the work • Resources required to do the work • Deliverables the project will (and will not) produce • Anticipated constraints in addressing the gap • Assumptions related to addressing the gap	1	2	2
Importance of closing the gap to others	• High—It's important to others that we address the gap • Moderate—It's somewhat important to others, or important to some of our stakeholders • Low—It's not very important to others	2	3	2
Anticipated consequences	• What are the potential consequences of addressing and not addressing the gap?	3	2	1
Magnitude	• What is the reach of the gap?	2	3	3
Costs	• High-level financial estimates of closing and not closing it • High-level nonfinancial estimates of closing and not closing it	2	1	2
Other alignment levels	• How would closing the gap affect other alignment levels? Other gaps? • How would not closing the gap affect other alignment levels? Other gaps?	2	1	2
Resources	• What resources are required to close the gap? • What resources would be consumed by not closing it?	1	3	2

Table 5-3. Gap Decision Criteria Scoring Worksheet

Name	Priority	Scope	Importance	Consequences	Magnitude	Costs	Levels	Resources
Jessie	3	1	2	3	2	2	2	1
Matt	3	2	3	2	3	1	1	3
Kristen	3	2	2	1	3	2	2	2
Total	**9**	**5**	**7**	**6**	**8**	**5**	**5**	**6**

With a shared understanding of the decision criteria, the group selected gaps that:
- were of high priority to the organization
- had the greatest reach within and outside the organization
- were highly important to the organization and its stakeholders.

Using this shared decision criteria, the team then negotiated the priority order and the number of gaps that could be addressed now. They considered questions such as what competing priorities may affect the number of gaps to select, as well as the timing of when each could be addressed, and if any of the gaps should be addressed together or in a sequential order. Kai's team identified four gaps to address immediately that met the most important shared criteria, and listed them in order of importance:

- -28 percent information accuracy
- -4 percent (A), -5 percent (B), -2 percent (C) agent satisfaction ratings
- +7 days wait time for processing
- +15 minutes time in queue.

Your team may also consider what to do about the gaps that were not selected for immediate solution. Will they be postponed? Monitored for a delayed decision? Abandoned entirely? Keep track of these gaps on your own, as well. As new problems and opportunities arise, you may be able to connect additional moving parts that are influencing performance in your organization. As new information becomes available through your continued strategic alignment work, the pressure points of the organization become more visible and allow you to do your job better and faster.

Now that you and your stakeholders have collaboratively identified which performance gaps to address, you can facilitate a shared understanding to determine the appropriate alignment level of these selected gaps. By doing this with your stakeholders, you will help the team select the most appropriate, and aligned, solution to the performance issue. Not only will your stakeholders be engaged in the decision making and implementation of solutions, but they will also share accountability for the results of your collaborative efforts.

Remember, with your systemic view, regardless of the alignment level of the performance gap, it has a relationship to the other levels. For example, the performance gap of "-5 agent to claims associate interactions per day" falls within the operational level with the number of interactions with a relationship to learning, organizational, and value-add results. As such, you must anticipate and account for the response to other levels of alignment.

Identifying Root Causes of Performance

With a negotiated understanding of the gaps you and your stakeholders will address (and the reasons supporting those shared decisions), your next step is to determine what is behind the performance gap the organization is experiencing. The effectiveness of your solution selection and implementation efforts are heavily contingent on uncovering the root cause of the performance problem. In other words, you must first determine the factors preventing or limiting the desired performance level.

To find root causes of performance problems you have to dig deeper. The problem the requestor is experiencing is likely the tip of the iceberg. Below the surface is where you'll find the opportunity to advance your strategic contribution; you'll reveal patterns and relationships across the organization that deal with culture and performance. As you dig deeper, you will be well positioned to select a solution that addresses the cause rather than the symptom. Here, your conversations will extend beyond how the organization is responding to the gaps to also include talking about what's causing this response. With that information, you have the best chance of picking the solution that has the best opportunity to succeed and avoid a wasteful use of resources, or even worse, performance results.

> Kai's team identified four gaps to address, each of which required thoughtful investigation into their root cause(s). Before meeting with the project team, Kai considered how to direct the conversation about uncovering root causes by thinking through the team's pick for the top gap: -28 percent information accuracy. Kai had a couple options for how to direct the conversation:

> **Meeting Option 1:**
> With the target gap identified (-28 percent information accuracy), the team would discuss potential solutions for closing the gap. Team members shared ideas for a solution, which were mostly ones the team was accustomed to using. The team decided a product training class would be the most effective for claims associates. Kai then started asking questions about implementing the solution: How many claims associates will receive the training? How long should the training be? What specific customer service topics should be covered?

> **Meeting Option 2:**
> With the target gap identified (-28 percent information accuracy), the team would discuss why the feedback score was below the target of 100 percent. Team members shared ideas about causes, which covered individual causes, such as claims associates are poorly motivated to do the work and this leads to errors, and environment causes, such as claims associates are receiving conflicting product information and this leads to errors. Team members calibrated their ideas, discussed how each may be influencing performance, and negotiated what would be required to make desired performance more attainable.

Meeting 1 is more typical of many work environments. Quick decisions mean quick action, and quick action is often rewarded. But notice that one slight change in the direction—from discussing solutions to discussing causes—can have a rewarding influence on the effectiveness and efficiency of the solution the team selects and on the dynamics and relationship L&D has with stakeholders.

> After these meetings, it was clear that Kai was making headway building a strategic partnership with Jessie. Kai was discussing gaps in performance and making collaborative decisions with other stakeholders about which gaps to address, as well as building knowledge about current business challenges, and growing confident that this team's decisions for solutions will meet those business needs.

Thomas Gilbert (1978), an industrial psychologist who studied under B.F. Skinner, highlighted the importance of considering both individual and environmental factors when examining performance in the workplace. You may hear a manager say "the employee is not motivated" or "just doesn't want to do it" when explaining why performance results are falling short. These assumptions place sole responsibility of the performance problem on the individual performer. However, Gilbert suggested that individual performance does not happen in a vacuum. Performance is the result of the interaction between the individual performer and her environment; therefore, when analyzing performance you must look at not only the performance of individuals, but also where and how that performance exists in the work environment.

Both individual and environmental factors contribute to performance, with environmental factors contributing the greatest barriers (Gilbert 1978). In fact, the workplace environment is the first place you should look, and it also happens to be where you have the most leverage for improvement.

Table 5-4 offers some lines of questioning that may identify the potential environmental and individual factors below the tip of the iceberg.

Table 5-4. Adapted Behavior Engineering Model

	Information	**Resources**	**Incentives**
Environmental Factors That Influence Performance	• Do employees know what is expected of them? • Are expectations clearly defined? • Do employees receive regular performance feedback? • Are work processes documented?	• Do employees have the tools, resources, and time necessary to perform to expectation? • Is written documentation of processes and procedures available to employees? • Are the work conditions conducive to the desired performance?	• Do employees have financial and nonfinancial incentives that reinforce desired performance? • Does the work enrich or fulfill employee needs? • Do employees believe there is an opportunity to succeed?
	Knowledge and Skills	**Capacity**	**Motives**
Individual Factors That Influence Performance	• Do employees have the necessary knowledge and skills to perform as desired? • Do employees have the opportunity to apply their knowledge and skills to the job?	• Do employees have the capacity to learn and perform as expected? • Are employees in the right position? On the right team? • Are the right employees recruited for the right positions?	• Are employee goals and organizational goals aligned? • Do employees have the desire to perform as expected?

Adapted from Chevalier (2002) and Gilbert (1978).

It was now Kai's team's turn to uncover the factors that were affecting (driving or inhibiting) performance. Using the root causes analysis template (Table 5-5), along with stakeholders, Kai identified the environmental and individual factors that underlie the target performance gap. To identify these factors, Kai started with the first gap, -28 percent information accuracy, and asked stakeholders, "Why do you think we are experiencing a gap of -28 percent in information accuracy?"

Once the stakeholder offered a response, Kai asked them to drill down further by asking "why?" multiple times:
- Response 1: Claims associates do not give consistent information to agents.
  - Why?
- Response 2: Claims associates use various product information resources.
  - Why?
- Response 3: Claims associates create their own job aids and documentation.
  - Why?
- Response 4: Work processes are not centrally documented or vetted.
  - Why?
- Response 5: Claims associates do not have access to an online workspace to share or view documented work processes.
  - Root cause.

Kai's team continued this process of asking why repetitively to drill down to the root cause of each performance gap. Because not all of the categories in the root cause analysis template were relevant, Kai's team only filled in the applicable identified root causes.

Table 5-5. Root Causes Analysis Template

	Information	Resources	Incentives
Environmental Factors That Influence Performance	Company policy information is not documented.	Claims associates do not have access to other company policies.	Employee professional development is limited.
	Knowledge and Skills	**Capacity**	**Motives**
Individual Factors That Influence Performance	Claims associates do not have knowledge of other company policy features and benefits.	Claims associates do not know how their position may be adjusted due to the acquisition.	

Now that your team has a good idea about what is under the surface and promoting or limiting performance, you can discuss how these identified drivers and barriers may be related and continue refining your shared understanding of the larger context of performance. A helpful tool to analyze these drivers and restraints of performance is Lewin's (1951) force field analysis. This tool is also useful for identifying the solution that will be necessary to move performance in the desired direction. For example, training as a solution cannot survive in the workplace on its own. In other words, you cannot train employees, put them back on the job, and expect their performance to magically improve. Other performance supports—such as line manager support with weekly feedback and changes to employee workload—may be necessary to achieve results at all levels of alignment.

Kai's team used the Force Field Analysis Worksheet (Table 5-6) to consider the drivers (those forces within the organization that help promote the desired performance) and the barriers (those forces that get in the way). This exercise helped the project team think through the realities of the working environment.

Kai's team listed the environmental and individual factors that promoted the desired performance on the left. Then, they rated the level of strength of the factor(s) by indicating +5 as the highest driving strength or 0 as neutral driving strength. Next, they listed the environmental and individual factors that prevented or limited the desired performance on the right. Finally, they rated the level of strength of the factors by indicating -5 as the highest restraining strength or 0 as neutral restraining strength.

Table 5-6. Force Field Analysis Worksheet

Driving Force (positive)	Force Strength											Restraining Force (negative)
	+5	+4	+3	+2	+1	0	-1	-2	-3	-4	-5	
Leadership support												New acquisition
Accessibility to resources												Existing workloads
Well-developed interdepartmental relationships												Staff Shortage

Adapted from Chevalier (2003).

You may opt to complete the force field analysis worksheet individually or as a team. In either case, it is important for team members to share their assumptions about what is driving and what is creating barriers to expected performance. With such a discussion, you can better determine the solution most appropriate to bring current performance up to desired levels.

As a team, review your responses and discuss how each of the identified factors is influencing performance, and what would be required to change the factor so that desired performance is more attainable. Remember, environmental factors have the greatest influence on performance; therefore, changes to these factors will have a greater chance of changing performance than individual factors.

Identifying Potential Solutions

You and your team of stakeholders are in a good position to make an informed decision about what solutions are most appropriate to address the performance problem or opportunity. You know what gaps are in performance, what factors are influencing that performance, and to what degree those factors are influencing performance. Now, you and your team are ready to determine appropriately aligned solutions.

To be sure the solution has the greatest chance for implementation, acceptance, and sustainability, it is a good practice to decide with your stakeholders what criteria you will use to make this important decision. Just as you did when collaboratively analyzing which gaps in performance to address with stakeholders, you should collaborate with stakeholders to identify and negotiate the criteria most important to them when making performance solution decisions.

See Table 5-7 for potential criteria to consider with your stakeholders when deciding on which solutions make the most sense given the evidence you have and the environment in which the solution will exist long term. In addition, ask your stakeholders:

- What criteria are most important to you?
- How important is each criterion you selected?

Table 5-7. Solution Selection Decision Criteria Checklist

Criterion	Defined	Scoring
Probability	What is the probability that this solution will close the gap?	3-High probability 2-Moderate probability 1-Low probability 0-No probability
Appropriateness	Does this solution make sense for our business, culture, and environment?	3-Very appropriate 2-Moderately appropriate 1-Somewhat appropriate 0-Not at all appropriate
Ability to support	What is the organizational ability to support the solution long term?	3-High ability 2-Moderate ability 1-Low ability 0-No ability
Barriers and constraints	What are the organizational barriers or constraints to implementing the solution long term?	3-No barriers or constraints 2-Low barriers or constraints 1-Moderate barriers or constraints 0-High barriers or constraints
Acceptability	What is the anticipated acceptance of those who will affect or be affected by the solution long term?	3-High acceptance 2-Moderate acceptance 1-Low acceptance 0-No acceptance
Time to implement	What is the anticipated total time required to implement the solution?	3-Time is not a concern 2-Time to implement is reasonable 1-Time to implement is a stretch but manageable 0-Time to implement is unreasonable
Cost to implement	What are the total costs of the solution (effort, time away from current work, maintenance)?	3-Below budget 2-Reasonable and within budget 1-A stretch, but manageable 0-Unreasonable, not doable

Kai knew the performance context was critical to the success of any solutions. In addition, understanding the criteria the stakeholders used to judge whether the solution "worked" was critical to the team's strategic relationship with the stakeholders. Even with positive improvements in results, stakeholders may think a solution didn't work if they are more concerned about whether the solution was too expensive, took too long, or faced resistance from staff. Kai used the solution decision criteria checklist and asked stakeholders to identify the score for each solution criterion. Kai then used the scoring worksheet in Table 5-8 to total the scores by category and assess the importance of each stakeholder. This exercise responded to the question, "What is the most important solution criteria according to the team?"

Table 5-8. Solution Decision Criteria Scoring Worksheet

Scorer	Probability	Appropriateness	Ability to Support	Barriers and Constraints	Acceptance	Time	Cost
Dana	2	1	3	2	0	2	1
Matt	3	1	2	1	2	0	3
Danielle	2	2	2	1	1	1	1
Kristen	1	2	0	1	2	1	2
Total	**8**	**6**	**7**	**5**	**5**	**4**	**7**

The team's preferred order suggests that the selected solution must:
- Have a high probability that it would specifically address the performance gap.
- Be something that the organization could support long term.
- Keep total costs of the solution at or below budget.
- Make some sense for the business, culture, and working environment.
- Have moderate to low organizational barriers or constraints to implement.
- Achieve moderate to low acceptance by those who would affect or be affected by the solution long term.
- Require a manageable amount of time to implement the solution.

From here, Kai's team was now able to explore potential solutions that fit the gap, as well as their shared decision criteria that facilitate successful implementation of the identified solutions using the same template design for analyzing the root cause of the performance problem.

The team identified collaborative solution options by inputting the selected solutions into the environmental and individual performance solutions template (Table 5-9). Kai's team did not identify a solution for every box in the template, so they were only included where applicable and when they fit with the team's shared decision criteria.

Table 5-9. Environmental and Individual Performance Solutions

	Information	Resources	Incentives
Environmental Performance Solutions	• Content knowledge management system • Weekly newsletter • Standard operating procedures	• Content knowledge management system • Printed job aids • Job shadowing	• Performance management and measurement system • Productivity bonuses
	Knowledge and Skills	**Capacity**	**Motives**
Individual Performance Solutions	• Content knowledge management system • Customer service training class	• Performance management system • Updated job descriptions	

Once you have some appropriate solution options to select from, you and your team can consider each carefully, specifically answering:

- What is the probability of each solution's overall potential to fit your environment and current circumstances?
- What is the organization's ability to support this solution long term?
- What are the high-level cost estimates to implement the solution long term?
- How appropriate is this solution to your business? Will it make sense to your stakeholders given your environment and current circumstances?
- What are the potential barriers and constraints that may inhibit the successful, long-term implementation of this solution?
- How likely are your stakeholders to accept this solution?
- What are the high-level estimates of time to implement the solution long term?

By reviewing and weighting the solution decision criteria collaboratively with clients, Kai made positive moves toward shared accountability with stakeholders and guided the team toward solution selections that made the most sense for the organization, taking the people, culture, and realities of the work environment into consideration.

During the discovery meetings, Kristen, the director of operations, expressed concerns about using resources for development purposes. She explained her hesitancy was in not funding "nice to haves," but she was very receptive to solutions that met documented business needs. By demonstrating the strategic process used to identify that a need does exist, the impact that problem may have should the need go unaddressed, and how the solution is aligned to the documented need, Kai could ensure alignment between the problem and solution and demonstrate the real strategic value of L&D contributions.

Using the solution options rubric (Table 5-10), Kai's team brainstormed many potential solutions and then reviewed each according to the shared decision-making criteria. Kai decided to include the initial request for a team-building training program in the analysis. Based on the team's shared solution decision criteria, Kai ranked the potential solutions in order in the first column. Team members responded to the question of "How closely does this solution meet the criteria?" by rating each solution on a scale of 0 to 3 (with 3 as the highest potential). Compiling all the scores from team members, Kai added the columns for each solution to identify the solutions with the greatest chance of success.

Table 5-10. Solution Options Rubric

	Solution 1: Content Knowledge Management System	Solution 2: Performance Management and Measurement System	Solution 3: Team-Building Training Class
Probability	3	3	1
Ability to Support	3	2	1
Cost to Implement	2	2	3
Appropriateness	3	3	1
Barriers and Constraints	2	1	2
Acceptability	3	2	2
Time to Implement	2	2	2
Chance of Success	18	15	12

After completing the rubric, Kai and the team determined that the first two solutions (developing a content knowledge management system and developing a performance management and measurement system) had the best chance of implementation success, given the performance gaps, support and barriers, shared solution criteria, and organizational realities. After the team reviewed the scores for the team-building training class, they agreed it was misaligned to the performance problem. This misalignment stemmed from challenges with resource allocation from senior leadership for a "development" solution, the current workload in the claims department, the inability of claims associates to take part in a solution that removes them from the job, and the importance of integrating the solution into the daily work of claims associates. With a decision in hand, Kai turned to negotiating the details of the implementation and execution of the solutions with all relevant stakeholders.

Align Solutions Checklist

Use the checklist below to ensure you have covered all elements necessary for successful demonstration of your ALIGN Solutions efforts.

Element of Alignment	Yes/No	How To
My System Thinking		
I outlined relationships and consequences for the various solutions	Y/N	
My Strategic Thinking		
I recommended appropriately aligned improvements to help the organization realize our desired results	Y/N	
I planned ahead by anticipating multiple scenarios and appropriate courses of action	Y/N	
My Critical Thinking		
I generated a reasoned method for selecting among several solution options	Y/N	
I applied metacognitive knowledge so that I could monitor my own performance	Y/N	
My Collaboration With Stakeholders		
I have communicated a commitment to foster teamwork and shared accountability for group decision making about the performance solution	Y/N	
I facilitated an openness to a variety of solutions	Y/N	
I presented coherent and persuasive arguments for controversial or difficult issues	Y/N	
I drove teamwork by recognizing and rewarding the achievement of goals, rather than individual performance	Y/N	
I established partnerships and reduced silo work by teaming up with other groups in the organization	Y/N	
I supported and committed to group decisions that fostered teamwork and shared accountability for our efforts	Y/N	

ALIGN Implementation

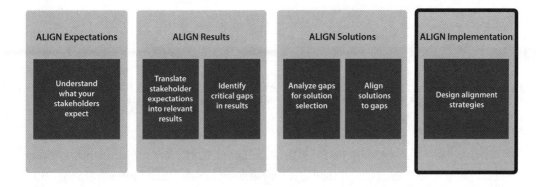

Your ALIGN Implementation efforts are aimed at making strategically aligned and collaborative decisions that identify transfer strategies for the solution, design implementation, and change management strategies to ensure successful execution and integration, as well as creating monitoring plans that keep pace with performance changes and alert you when adjustments are needed. With consensus of the solution selection criteria in hand, you can now agree on the solution recommendations with your stakeholders.

To ensure the long-term success and survival of the selected solution, you will collaboratively derive an implementation plan with your stakeholders. This includes planning how to manage the desired change in performance, designing transfer strategies that integrate the change into employees' daily repertoire, designing implementation strategies to map the work flow that integrates the change into the organization, identifying performance measures that facilitate the ongoing assessment of the change, and establishing communication strategies for the life cycle of the change. Table 6-1 lists objectives to accomplish and activities to help you meet them.

Table 6-1. ALIGN Implementation Objectives and Activities

Objectives to Accomplish	Activities Designed to Meet the Objectives
• Design change management strategies • Identify and design transfer strategies • Design implementation strategies	• Derive thoughtful change management strategies to facilitate integration of your performance improvement work
• Identify performance measures that will supply ongoing performance feedback • Design communication strategies	• Design a monitoring plan to ensure regular performance feedback • Collaboratively negotiate communication strategy of performance feedback
• Conduct an ongoing reflection of your work	• Ongoing review of the ALIGN Implementation checklist to assess your performance

Planning for Change Creation and Management

Any performance change designed and implemented in the organization has a direct effect on people. As such, change management strategies must take human response into account. For example, if you are introducing a change to the documentation of work expectations, how will this change affect job roles and responsibilities? How will introducing or altering standard operating procedures change the way employees use technology? How will it affect daily responsibilities? How will it affect employee morale?

When a change is introduced, employees often look to the leaders when assessing expectations of performance to provide direction, support, and role modeling. Are all leaders aligned and committed to the change? How do employees know? Are leaders modeling the change? Are they rewarding and recognizing the change in others? Can leaders speak to and champion the experience and remove barriers to support the effort required to sustain long-term change?

While leadership and management support is necessary, it is critical to establish ownership of the change at all levels in the organization, especially individual employees who experience the day-to-day consequences of the change. There are a handful of practices that you and the project team may engage in to facilitate the long-term integration and success of performance improvement solutions, including:

- **Designing transfer strategies**—Purposefully consider how the solution will be applied, supported, and integrated into the daily routine of the workforce.
- **Designing implementation strategies**—Purposefully plan solution implementation details, such as refining the scope of the project, securing commitment to resources, and crafting a deployment plan.

- **Identifying performance measures**—Negotiate with your stakeholders what data will be collected to measure performance.
- **Monitoring the change in performance**—With performance measures in hand, negotiate the details of a monitoring plan with your stakeholders.
- **Deriving a communication strategy**—Don't let your project "die on the vine"; collaboratively decide who will get project information, how often, and when.

Designing Transfer Strategies

Transfer strategies speak to the specific efforts made to ensure successful application and integration of the solution on the job. Burke and Hutchins (2008) surveyed performance improvement practitioners to determine successful strategies for implementing and integrating performance support solutions into the workplace. Practitioners noted that particular emphasis should be placed on the environment in which the solution will live. This aligns with industrial psychologist Thomas Gilbert's thinking that the environment plays a bigger role than the individual in performance. Practitioners may apply this critical component by coordinating the delivery and implementation of the solution as close together as possible. For example, provide training to employees at the time they are going to be able to apply that training to the job. This may affect how training is rolled out (to whom and the order of training delivery).

Other successful transfer strategies rest within the training design and delivery phases, much of which is within your control. For example, you have a working knowledge and an appreciation for how the solution, the employee, and the environment will interact. You can apply this knowledge by accounting for environmental realities (such as time to use the solution on the job or reinforcement of desired behaviors on the job) in the design and delivery of the solution.

The implementation plan should also account for the time to transition from the old way to the new way, acknowledging that the performance of an employee will not change overnight. For example, you shouldn't expect an employee to look and perform differently right after attending a training class. The performance will transform over time, so a transition plan will serve the expectations well.

> Kai's team decided to develop a content knowledge management system and a performance management and measurement system because they believed the solutions were aligned to the documented performance gaps and met the solution selection criteria. They next considered strategies that would be important to ensuring that the selected solutions had the best chance of success before, during, and after implementation.

There are a variety of transfer strategies that you may employ to foster successful implementation and sustainability of the solution. The strategy or strategies you select are grounded in the context of performance within the organization. In other words, you and your stakeholders will select transfer strategies that are best suited to the internal and external conditions of performance. The following are examples of transfer strategies for before, during, and after implementation:

- **Before Implementation:**
  - Prepare transfer environment to align with expected changes in performance (such as policies, procedures, and structures).
  - Orient supervisors (and others) to the solution, expectations of performance, and shared accountability for results.

- **During Implementation:**
  - Build in time for practice and testing.
  - Reinforcement and rewards.
  - Provide regular feedback.
  - Derive action plans for commitment.
  - Provide support tools for using the solutions on the job (such as job aids and checklists).
  - Maintain and communicate high expectations.

- **After Implementation:**
  - Measure and monitor changes in performance.
  - Plan, coordinate, and facilitate regular stakeholder follow-ups.
  - Incentivize stakeholders for continuous improvement.
  - Coordinate coaching or other support during transition (such as learning support groups).
  - Publicize and communicate progress and successes.

Kai's team collaboratively developed their list of timing and sample transfer strategies. The team then identified specific tasks and activities that would ensure their list of identified transfer strategies were applied. They then began considering the details surrounding implementing these solutions. For example, how would the team prepare the claims department for successful implementation of the content knowledge management system before the system was developed? How would the team orient claims supervisors about the expectations of using the performance management and measurement system? Kai documented their negotiations of successful activities aimed at driving successful implementation (Table 6-2).

Table 6-2. Successful Implementation Activities

Solution	Before Implementation	During Implementation	After Implementation
Corporate Knowledge Management System (CKMS)	• Assemble SME committee • Create committee charter • Assemble product knowledge tools, marketing materials, and policy documents • Attend information technology meetings related to the CKMS's design and development	• Conduct pilot testing of CKMS • Compile, review, and approve product knowledge tools • Compile, review, and approve product information pages • Provide weekly productivity results to claims department	• Facilitate lessons-learned meetings • Publish product knowledge tools • Provide quarterly productivity and satisfaction results to stakeholder group • Provide recommendations for continuous improvement

Performance Measurement and Management System (PMMS)	• Champion the modeling of how to integrate people and process in the organization
	• Document HR processes:
	  ° Hiring
	  ° Exit Interviews
	  ° Compensation
	  ° Job Analysis
	  ° Design and develop PMMS
		• Integrate job roles, responsibilities, and compensation
		• Pilot test PMMS
			• Facilitate lessons-learned meetings
			• Plan for Phase 2, where focus is on scaling the PMMS across the organization
			• Provide quarterly productivity and satisfaction results to stakeholder group
			• Provide recommendations for continuous improvement

Table 6-3 provides some items to consider when designing for transfer, with corresponding sample transfer strategies that facilitate successful and sustainable implementation. While these questions are useful for any context, the sample transfer strategies you select collaboratively with your stakeholders will vary according to your performance context.

Once your group has committed to the decisions, you can work out the design and delivery of the solution. Designing the solution is also a collaborative endeavor involving representatives from those who will affect or be affected by the solution on the job. Delivery of the solution may be the task of one person, a team, or a collaborative effort.

Table 6-3. Sample Transfer Strategies

Transfer Considerations	Transfer Strategies
How will the solution be used on the job?	• New or expanded work assignments
How will the solution be supported on the job?	• Coaching, mentoring, feedback, job shadowing
What are the anticipated supports and barriers of the solution being used on the job?	• Information, expectations communicated, resources, incentives
What are the employees' opportunities to use and integrate the solution on the job?	• Immediate or delayed use of solution on the job • Frequent or infrequent use of solution on the job
Who are the SMEs for this solution, if applicable?	• Who will be available for support when using the solution on the job?
What is the plan for the design of the solution?	• Who will lead the design? • Who else is involved? • Who should be involved?
What is the deployment plan for the solution?	• Who will lead the delivery? • Who else is involved? • Who should be involved?
How often will you follow up with stakeholders after the solution is implemented?	• Testing the design and delivery of the solution • Immediately following implementation of the solution • At what intervals following implementation of the solution?
How will you follow up with those who are using the solution on the job? How will you monitor its progress?	• Observation • Questionnaire • Informal feedback from users • Feedback from customers • Focus groups
How and when will you communicate progress with stakeholders?	• Email • Face-to-face • Quarterly status reports
What tasks are required to implement the solution?	• Project tasks (e.g., design the solution, deliver the solution, test the solution)
How will you cascade the solutions?	• Implement one solution at a time • Implement the solutions in bundles • Connect with another initiative

Designing Implementation Strategies

With your transfer strategies in hand, you can now move to planning the implementation of the selected solution. It is necessary to consider how and when the solution will be carried out, who will be responsible for what parts of carrying out the solution, how you might sequence the rollout of the solution, and other details that ensure successful and sustainable implementation of the solution. Details you may consider include:

- **Scope of the initiative work.** Project scope tells you the boundaries of the work that will be (and will not be) performed. Scope includes identifying and documenting project details such as the project objectives, goals, phases and deliverables, timelines, budget, resources, and schedule. (Tip! Be a scope creep buster! Be sure to have your project team and stakeholders sign off on the project scope.)

- **Solution requirements.** Solution requirements define the capabilities required to achieve the project goals and objectives. By defining solution requirements, you will gain an understanding of the best way to integrate the solution on the job while balancing both environmental and human requirements. These requirements bring to light the conditions necessary for successful and effective adoption and integration of your solution. Consider the environmental and human factors that may need to be altered so that your solution is aligned. What must be built, designed, modified, eliminated, or reduced to deliver the solution?

- **Commitment for resources.** Resources are what's necessary to carry out the project successfully, such as people, budget, or tools. Document the resources that will be required to carry the project from initiation through the life cycle of the project.

- **Solution design.** Solution design includes the design, development, and testing of the solution. As with all other aspects of the process, solution design must be conducted collaboratively with your stakeholders (those who will affect and be affected by the solution) and must be designed in alignment with your solution requirements.

- **Deployment plan.** Your deployment plan lays out the logistics of the project implementation. For example, who will receive the solution? How will it be received? When will it be received? For how long? What is your cascading plan? How, if at all, does the solution interact with existing priorities or projects?

It is very likely that your organization has many other critical projects in various life cycle stages right now. Some projects are just getting off the ground, while some are in the implementation phase. It is important for your stakeholders to not see this as just another fad or as a project that counteracts other initiatives. As such, you and your project team may consider the environment in which the solutions will live and how they may interact with that environment. Some other items to consider include:

- How many recommendations can be managed at one time?
- What, if any, are the organization's competing priorities that may affect the solution's execution?
- What other organizational initiatives may be happening concurrently with your solutions?

- How will the recommendations affect resource availability throughout the project life cycle?
- What other solutions have been implemented in the past? What were the results? What were the lessons learned?

Next, you will engage your stakeholders in a conversation about the priority of executing the chosen solutions. It may be that the organization can handle implementing only one or two of the solutions at any one time, due to other factors that may affect the success of the solution, such as the timing, workloads of affected staff, or competing priorities. Use the following list as a guide to determine the prioritization, or cascading, of implementing the solutions.

- **First Priority:**
  - Critical organizational issues that offer the greatest impact to the highest alignment level
- **Second Priority:**
  - Solution(s) that alter existing organizational practices that can be quickly adopted and build momentum for solution(s) to follow
- **Third Priority:**
  - Improvements to work processes or procedures
- **Fourth Priority:**
  - Improvements to worker skills, capacities, engagement

Kai's team decided to move forward with both solutions simultaneously. The team believed the groups responsible for carrying out the tasks of designing, developing, and delivering the solutions (namely, information technology, human resources, and the claims department) were on board, and that the leadership team was ready to provide the resources to move ahead. The team also considered the execution culture of the organization, specifically its emphasis on efficiency, effectiveness, and timeliness. Working on the two selected solutions concurrently allowed the team to expedite processes, combine resources, and promote collaborative work.

Kai and the team further confirmed their selected implementation strategies and negotiated their roles and expectations as the team began the first stages of solution design. Kai also negotiated the monitoring plan with stakeholders by referencing their completed data collection template, connecting to the initial gaps in results that the team had identified. Kai also recommended considering additional indicators. For example, in addition to using the annual employee engagement score to assess employee engagement, the team could also consider other intermediate indicators that would tell them whether the solution was on track, and to increase their opportunity to make adjustments before the solution had the desired impact. The team agreed that collecting these data would be informative, allow for more timely insight, and be relatively easy to obtain from HR's exit interview data, thus providing richer insight into employee engagement levels. The chief of administration added overtime dollars as another intermediate indicator that would give insight into how the solution was working.

Kai then updated the data collection template and included space for monitoring the results, and put reminders on the team calendar to compile and analyze the data, reflect on the results and opportunities for continuous improvement, and share the results with stakeholders according to scheduled and agreed-upon times.

Agreeing on Performance Measures

Before implementing your solution, it is wise to agree on the performance measures that will be used to monitor performance improvements over time. Don't wait for the solution to be in place for a while before determining your monitoring and evaluation plan! In each of the prior stages of the strategic alignment process, you obtained information about what performance measures would be appropriate for assessing employee performance after the solution is in place (both from the perception of stakeholders and tangible results at various levels). This information may be organized according to the four alignment levels. Table 6-4 provides an example of results at each alignment level and sample performance measures.

Table 6-4. Sample Performance Measures for Each Alignment Level

Alignment Level	Result	Sample Performance Measures
Value-Add	Aligning solutions to the needs of external clients, society, or the community	• Customer satisfaction • Mortality rate • Access to care • Access to education • Gross domestic product • Employment rate • Crime rate
Business	Aligning solutions to the organization's bottom line	• Year-over-year sales • Annual profits • Net promoter score • Customer retention, acquisition cost, or complaints • First contact resolution • Employee turnover rate • Time to fill positions • Employee satisfaction
Performance	Aligning solutions with specific accomplishments of a person or a group	• Leads generated • Sales cycle • Project cycle time • Delivery on-time rate
Learning	Aligning solutions with how work is done	• Errors and defects • Process improvements • Efficiency rate

Kai continued to shape realistic expectations by reiterating to stakeholders that deploying the solutions was not the end of the interaction between L&D and the challenges in the claims department that started this collaborative work. Kai emphasized that the aligned solutions are strategic investments in the organization, and, as such, require ongoing check-ins to ensure that the decisions made were sound and to inform future decisions. Using a collaborative approach, Kai derived performance measures that would be used to monitor performance improvements over time.

The data gathered and used from monitoring were framed as evidence to support decision making and inform if and when to make enroute modifications. By using monitoring data, Kai also continued to forge a strategic relationship with stakeholders by providing timely evidence and encouraging the use of that evidence when making decisions about how to respond to performance problems or opportunities. Kai promoted a shared accountability of the results generated by the selected solutions, all while demonstrating the strategic value of L&D work.

Monitoring Performance Change

Monitoring and evaluation (M&E) can provide a systemic and systematic framework that aligns decisions, results, activities, and resources so that performance data is responsive and provides a clear recipe for improving performance (Guerra-López 2008). Such alignment sets the stage for relevant and ongoing performance feedback, which sheds light on the progress an organization is making toward (or away from) its vision and related measurable objectives. Thus, this ongoing feedback obtained through a well-designed (that is, well-aligned) monitoring and evaluation system is a fundamental element of continuous improvement.

In the last half-century, learning and development has turned to monitoring and evaluation as a means of supporting continuous improvement, although its progress has been slow (Wang and Spitzer 2005). One explanation may be that current evaluation approaches measure the effects of a single solution with results reported at the individual employee level, at one point in time. This approach does not account for the complexity of organizations and the ability to detect, influence, and report impact at the organizational level. A holistic perspective is required, one that integrates the M&E process into a broader organizational performance system, and looks beyond the solution's most immediate effects (Guerra-López 2010; Wang and Spitzer 2005). This systemic view gives you the ability to detect patterns from the data to understand internal and external factors for change, and subsequently select appropriate courses of action (Grieves 2003). If this type of integration is achieved, L&D can become a proactive partner in supporting evidenced-based decision making that results in continuous performance improvement.

To support this growth to strategic partner, a continuous improvement approach to performance improvement may be applied. A business unit that is strategically aligned applies four key dimensions to its work:

- **They gather evidence.** While fundamental to responsible decision making, the most neglected aspect of decision making in the literature is intelligence gathering (Eisenhardt 1998; Nutt 2007). Decision making begins when stakeholders see a triggering trend (for example, declining revenues or sales) or event (for example, a threat to unionize) as significant, prompting steps to obtain intelligence (Nutt 2007). Decision makers are often inundated with signals from customers, employees, shareholders, attorneys, competitors, regulators, and suppliers. Finding which trends or events are worthy of priority attention can be an overwhelmingly challenging proposition. A strategically aligned partner gathers evidence to identify gaps in performance and uses that evidence to make decisions about the weights of performance challenges or opportunities that are continually presented on the job.

- **They monitor evidence.** Monitoring integrates measurement and tracking: measuring what matters and tracking its progress. Continual improvement depends on knowing where you are headed, and constantly monitoring your course to get you from where you are to where you want to be (Guerra-López 2007). You do this by asking the right questions, continually collecting useful data, and then using that information to make sound decisions about required changes and which current programs to sustain. With this continuous and proactive approach, organizations focus on their performance targets and align efforts toward these goals, creating value for the organization.

- **They use evidence.** One of the critical contributions of monitoring and evaluation is the feedback that it provides. The feedback loop represents the reiterative nature of tracking and adjusting. Open communication of the evaluation process, findings, and recommendations directly influences the change process. Lack of information promotes a sense of anxiety and resistance, particularly when individuals begin to make their own stories about what is going on and what will happen in the future. This feedback is provided by monitoring facilitates an ongoing dialogue with stakeholders in which we can empower them to have performance data readily accessible to those affected. Providing consistent feedback about performance is part of a broader, more effective communication system. If developed appropriately, it will allow leaders and employees to track, manage, and sometimes forecast performance at opportune times. In this sense, it is very much like monitoring the vital signs of the organization.

- **They learn from evidence.** The benefit of continual improvement can have great payoffs in any endeavor. The ideal process is one that can be controlled to define and then maintain quality, and to adjust at the earliest sign that something is not acceptable. While quality control measures keep things on track, all parts of the organization are encouraged to look, in a coordinated fashion, for ways to improve the enterprise by adjusting design specifications and altering the various processes to include any new improved features and changing that which will not deliver measurable success. Decisions regarding adjustments or change tactics are made daily. Pound (1995) warns these subtle day-to-day decisions are where we are most susceptible to organizational failure. Daily decisions may include: "Is the rate of progress obtained consistent with the rate of progress planned?" "How has the solution affected individual areas and the system?" "Is the solution and its results sustainable?" "Why or why not?" Ongoing performance data are required to inform these adjustment decisions. L&D functions seeking the ultimate level of continuous improvement identify means of developing systematic processes grounded in systemic views and gain the opportunity to effectively and efficiently monitor progress, and therefore, alignment to the organization.

The value of monitoring is not in using it as a means of control or to stifle creativity or innovation. Wells, Moorman, and Werner (2007) demonstrated that employees have a positive response to monitoring activities when reasons for the activity are understood and trusted as means for development. Gruman and Saks (2011) argue that including employees in the development of goals supports employee engagement, which leads to desired performance with both the employee and the organization as benefactors. Such practices allow employees to situate their goals within the organizational context and welcome a collaborative monitoring design.

The process of monitoring does not imply you forgo a summative confirmation and celebration of ultimate results. With the direction to continuously monitor progress, organizations are encouraged to identify milestone opportunities that acknowledge improvements and time to reflect on what worked well that should be repeated and what improvements should be made for the future. "Progress, milestones reached (or not reached), action plans for reaching desired goals, etc. should be consistently and accurately communicated throughout the organization" (Guerra-López 2008). A discussion on where you've been, a description and acknowledgment of the efforts that have led to the progress, and how you will continue to move forward to achieve your goal is recommended at specified intervals.

Kai used continuous and transparent communication to develop trusting and strategic relationships with stakeholders. After Kai's team developed a shared monitoring plan, Kai guided the team to outline communication strategies. The monitoring plan established expectations for what data to collect, where the data would come from, and how often the data would be reviewed. Then, the team negotiated whom the results would be communicated to, how often to share results, and how. The team also considered allocating time for the core project team to check in and reflect on current, trending, and projected results. Kai kept track of how these ongoing feedback and reflection meetings were used to inform stakeholders' decision making, which kept Kai informed on not only stakeholder decision making, but also changes in organizational performance over time.

Establishing Communication Strategies

Throughout the project, you facilitated participation from your stakeholders, determining and calibrating performance expectations, weighting and prioritizing performance gaps, and deriving solutions that were aligned to the performance gaps. You maintained superior communication throughout, and it's not time to stop now.

Your ongoing communication makes the case for why the change in performance is required. You are articulating the need for the change, demonstrating faith that the organization can and will achieve its goals, and describing the picture of what individual and shared benefits will come from the change.

This communication takes on many forms. It may be in the form of a status report that communicates the current status of the solution, identifies significant accomplishments, or describes the activity or scheduled projects that are underway. Or it may be a project plan to communicate the tasks, owners, and status along the way.

To ensure everyone remained on the same page, Kai created a communication planner to negotiate what communications should be made, by whom, when, and for what purposes throughout the life cycle of the solution (Table 6-5).

Kai's approach to business alignment was central to changing the expectations and accountabilities of the L&D department. Kai applied a strategic and collaborative method to understanding the expectations of stakeholders, using evidence to inform where the organization wanted to be compared with where it currently was, selecting solutions that were aligned to the gaps in results, and negotiating plans to ensure sustainability of those solutions. Kai's strategic approach to Jessie's business problem improved the perceptions and utility of L&D work as strategically valuable. At last, Kai developed a reputation as a colleague who can guide partners to solutions that make sense for the business—and generate business results that matter.

Table 6-5. Communication Planner

Owner	What	Why	Who Receives	When and How
Jessie	Overall project updates	To provide ongoing status of the project	• Project sponsor • Project team • Leadership team	Project team meeting agendas and minutes are emailed within two business days of monthly project meetings.
Matt	Design and development of SOPs	To provide ongoing status of solution design and development	• Technical writing team • Project sponsor • Project team • Leadership team • Project leader	Technical writing team weekly summaries are emailed to relevant parties on Friday afternoons.
Danielle and Kai	Performance measures	To provide ongoing monitoring of solution performance measures	• Project sponsor • Project team • Leadership team • Project leader • Management team • End users	Performance reports are emailed quarterly.
Kristen	Project implementation updates	To provide ongoing status of implementation efforts	• Project sponsor • Project team • Leadership team • Management team • Project leader • Technical writing team • End users	Implementation updates are provided in regular monthly project meetings for nonurgent issues. Urgent issue updates are provided as needed with direct phone contact to the project sponsor and project leader.

ALIGN Implementation Checklist

Use the checklist below to ensure you have covered all elements necessary for successful demonstration of your stage three efforts.

Element of Alignment	Yes/No	How To
My System Thinking		
I am able to make sense of how the change will influence performance at multiple levels in the organization	Y/N	
I am able to determine what will help desired performance happen	Y/N	
I was able to determine what may get in the way of desired performance	Y/N	
My Strategic Thinking		
I did an objective analysis by investigating what, when, why, where, and how	Y/N	
I thought about how the people, processes, and structures will change	Y/N	
My Critical Thinking		
I recommended strategies for use of the solution on the job	Y/N	
Collaboratively, a monitoring plan was developed to track the solution	Y/N	
I explored the short-term and long-term outcomes of the solution	Y/N	
I am able to forecast the impact of the solution	Y/N	
My Collaboration With Stakeholders		
I presented coherent and persuasive arguments for controversial or difficult issues	Y/N	
I used my effective listening skills to better under-stand value from the perspectives of my stakeholders	Y/N	
I established partnerships and reduced silo work by teaming up with other groups in the organization	Y/N	
I supported and committed to group decisions that fostered teamwork and shared accountability for our efforts	Y/N	
I negotiated the next course of action with my stakeholders	Y/N	

Strategically Aligning the L&D Function

The more closely employees that perceive solutions are aligned to the strategic direction of the organization, the more likely these solutions are to be incorporated on the job, resulting in a stronger commitment to organizational strategy. This represents a fruitful avenue for learning and development to demonstrate its strategic influence to the organization (Montesino 2002). Chapter 2 made the distinction between the reactive and proactive alignment of learning and development, in which it is responding to performance problems—or it is preemptively designing the L&D function through underlying structures, supporting mechanisms, and activities that make it operate as an organizational strategic execution function. Strategically aligning the L&D function provides a way to proactively integrate what it does to generate strategic value.

While some L&D functions have been successful in achieving alignment, it is rare. L&D strategic alignment may not be clearly understood because the underlying elements and factors associated with facilitating successful L&D strategic alignment aren't clearly articulated. L&D functions that assume the responsibility of stewardship of human performance in organizations take a proactive position in linking performance data, decisions, actions, and results. The learning and development function may not only improve the perceptions of its strategic value, but also contribute to its purpose of developing human capital by modeling how and why such practices are critical to strategy development and execution. L&D performance may then be derived from the degree to which it achieves alignment and, ultimately, delivers strategic value to stakeholders.

L&D Functional Alignment and Organizational Performance

Continuous performance improvement requires timely, accurate, and actionable performance data to support organizational decision making. To aid decision making, L&D professionals must set out to understand in what ways its work may directly or indirectly affect organizational performance. The relationship is measured by the direct effects of L&D operations and outputs on organizational outcomes, reflecting current evaluation trends of program measurement for training and nontraining solutions. While useful for specific program feedback, it does not take the integrated, synergistic influence of learning and development into account, and it has been challenging to isolate the effects of training and its impact on performance (ASTD 2009).

A measurement approach used to remedy this limitation is the indirect, dynamic approach to measurement, which looks at the fit between the L&D function and organizational strategy. As an example of an indirect measure, training has been demonstrated to influence outcomes such as employee turnover, ultimately affecting the organization's financial results (Singh et al. 2012; Van Iddekinge et al. 2009).

As argued throughout this book, strategic alignment may be viewed as a process that enables companies and functions to be more effective. For learning and development, the examination of alignment can yield valuable, predictive information regarding the relationships between L&D systems and business performance (Chan et al. 1997). For example, it may identify the strengths and weaknesses of L&D, and the utility provided to stakeholders. So while achieving strategic alignment does not guarantee improved organizational performance, it does mean organizational leaders will consider alignment as one of many tools that can be used to gain and sustain competitive advantage.

Thus, the goal is not to strive for perfect alignment, but rather to engage in the processes that facilitate ongoing alignment, beyond strategic planning to ongoing strategic execution. Alignment is thus not only an end state but also an ongoing process. Reaching an ideal state of strategic alignment requires constant pursuit to keep pace with changes as shifts in strategic priorities require different employee behaviors, skills, and knowledge.

L&D Alignment as a System Change

Both proactive and reactive approaches to alignment are critical, complementary, and rest on system change methods because everything within the organizational system exists as it does due to the complex set of recurrent patterns of cause and effect. Therefore, whether you are trying to fix a specific performance problem or your aim is to position the L&D

function to support new strategic opportunities, how you go about it has to reflect a system perspective of change.

While we recognize that organizations are part of a broader societal system, at this point we are focusing specifically on the organization as the target system. System change takes place in multiple dimensions and may involve:

- shifting the components of the system or their sequence
- shifting interactions between the components of the system
- altering the whole through shifts in underlying choices and routines
- shifting how the system generates and uses feedback to improve itself.

As with everything in a system, these dimensions are interconnected so that change in one supports changes in all others. System change is a journey that can require a radical change in people's attitudes as well as in the ways people work. The L&D function aims to bring about lasting change by altering underlying structures and supporting mechanisms that make the system operate in a particular way. They can include expectations, policies, routines, relationships, resources, power structures and values, feedback mechanisms, skills and behaviors, and incentives and rewards, among many other mechanisms.

L&D Functional Alignment Framework

Geary Rummler and Brache (1995) identified nine performance variables that account for the multiple levels and dimensions of performance that exist within a system, all of which are critical to analyzing issues of alignment within organizations (Table 7-1). The three levels of performance are organization, process, and performer. To effect change in organizations, it is necessary to address the effects of the change on all three levels. For example, implementing change to drive the strategic alignment of the L&D function could mean significant changes to the job responsibilities and the skills of L&D members required to execute the strategic alignment efforts. Not accounting for these interrelationships may result in failed process implementation. Clear goals, at each level, are required to allow for appropriate alignment with an organization's desired results. Design refers to how the structure is arranged in ways that facilitate achievement of the goals. And management refers to the various practices performed to ensure goals are being achieved.

The proactive charge of the L&D function is to drive and develop performance within. To fulfill this charge, Rummler and Brache's performance variables may be applied as a lens to guide the strategic alignment of the L&D function in your organization. They have also been used as a framework for a diagnostic tool to determine the level of alignment of the L&D function.

Table 7-1. The 9 Performance Variables

	Goals	Design	Management
Organization	Strategy, operating plans, and metrics	Organization structure and overall business model	Performance review practices and management culture
Process	Customer and business requirements	Process design, systems design, and workspace design	Process ownership, process management, and continuous improvement
Performer	Job specifications, performance metrics, and individual development plans	Job roles and responsibilities, skill requirements, procedures, tools, and training	Performance feedback, consequences, coaching, and support

Adapted from Rummler and Brache (1995)

L&D Alignment Diagnostic

Linking the L&D function to organizational strategies requires a list of specific processes and behaviors. The L&D Strategic Alignment Scale (Hicks 2016) is an empirically validated scale that consists of the most significant elements for L&D strategic alignment. The tool has been validated by L&D practitioners and experts with a wide range of expertise and levels of experience.

The diagnostic questionnaire lists the L&D skills and behaviors identified as most critical to the strategic alignment and contributions of learning and development (Table 7-2). The questionnaire is followed by a thorough discussion of its contents and their importance to L&D strategic alignment.

Strategically aligned L&D teams are perceived to have a firm grasp on what the emerging needs of the business are, and can communicate how their decisions for solutions meet those needs. They communicate this message confidently using business language, both in written and verbal communications with stakeholders. They know the company's value chain and how their work connects and demonstrates value to the business.

The L&D team must also be able to speak confidently with line managers about the emerging business needs and discussions of how to best to meet them, effectively and efficiently. Business skills also play a role in how the L&D strategy is communicated. The L&D strategic plan is written in business language and offers strong evidence for the business case for learning decisions. Members of the L&D function must be able to perform gap analysis and synthesize the results to form connections at the operational, tactical, and strategic levels of the organization. Making these connections throughout the performance system is the key to a strategically aligned L&D function.

Learning and development must strike a balance of value to be delivered to its internal customers and external stakeholders (Rummler and Brache 2010). When considering making value connections to the organizational performance system, L&D must begin with the value that is delivered to the external customer and then consider the value to be delivered to the internal stakeholder. This is where the strategically driven links start—outward, then inside the organization. This focus shifts the attention away from short-term gains that may be delivered to internal stakeholders (at the expense of other parts of the system). Learning and development must move its attention beyond functional preferences, ad hoc requests, or silo approaches to work to make connections beyond the activity or output levels.

Table 7-2. L&D Alignment Diagnostic

Item	Strongly Disagree	Disagree	Somewhat Agree	Agree	Strongly Agree
1. L&D understands the emerging needs of the business	1	2	3	4	5
2. L&D knows the business value chain	1	2	3	4	5
3. L&D has confidence to speak in business terms to line executives	1	2	3	4	5
4. L&D strategic execution plans are communicated in business language	1	2	3	4	5
5. L&D understands the context in which the business operates	1	2	3	4	5
6. L&D is deeply aware of what is necessary to execute a firm's strategies	1	2	3	4	5
7. L&D understands how its efforts are linked to the organization's mission	1	2	3	4	5
8. L&D provides ongoing communication of the business case for solutions or initiatives	1	2	3	4	5
9. The L&D function works proactively with line managers to develop trust	1	2	3	4	5
10. There is an internal climate of cooperation where the learning function can exercise its role in creating strategic alignment	1	2	3	4	5
11. L&D receives support from line managers	1	2	3	4	5
12. The L&D function plans how interventions will be integrated throughout the organization.	1	2	3	4	5
13. Just-in-time learning solutions are offered to address current business needs	1	2	3	4	5
14. The learning function has ongoing dialogue with line managers	1	2	3	4	5
15. Gap analysis is performed to inform the design and delivery of strategic interventions	1	2	3	4	5

L&D teams are perceived to understand the context in which the business operates. As such, they should be shaped according to organizational needs rather than L&D needs. L&D practitioners must have the skills necessary to perform the critical internal strategic processes, which places them in the position of having current, working information of the emerging needs of the business. With this information, L&D can form a theory of impact by reverse engineering value from the external view of the customer and working inward from impact, outcomes, outputs, and activities. Rummler and Brache (2010) describe this approach as a necessity to "think differently about the contribution of work." In other words, learning and development must plan the design and management of the function toward the value creation system with effective and efficient use of resources.

The communication of how learning and development approaches its work is also an essential ingredient in the perception of its strategic alignment. Learning and development can share their value creation opportunities and successes in verbal and written forms of ongoing communication. Strategically aligned learning and development has the skill and ability to speak confidently in business terms with line executives and managers about business issues; for example, the gap between the capabilities of employees and the requirements to meet strategic priorities. Where are you now? Where do you want to be? These L&D functions monitor critical organizational issues such as the current priorities of the organization, and the future desired state of the organization (Anderson 2008). Strategically aligned learning and development can describe this gap in results and offer human performance solutions that make sense for the business. They demonstrate an awareness of what it will take to execute strategies and offer vivid descriptions of what the company will look like once the priorities are carried out. They will also proactively seize opportunities to provide ongoing communication about the business case for their decisions. They recognize that these decisions are investments in the organization and—like any other company investment that requires a commitment of funding and resources—can offer credible evidence of the soundness of the decision.

Cooperation also has a significant presence in this diagnostic questionnaire. A cooperative relationship specifies that the L&D function is proactive and purposeful when developing trusting relationships with line managers. It needs an internal climate of cooperation to exercise its role in creating strategic alignment within the organization, which requires support from line managers. Cooperation allows L&D to plan for how learning solutions will be integrated throughout the organization and to provide just-in-time solutions aimed at current business needs. The cooperation factor describes the type of relationship internal customers require from the L&D function. Strategically aligned L&D functions take the lead in the relationship to develop trust and to identify what measures the stakeholder uses to determine value.

Through this, L&D can establish the value expectations of internal stakeholders and offer solutions that meet those expectations. These L&D functions work closely with line managers—who are looking for quick learning solutions that are well integrated throughout the organization—to establish ongoing dialogue and perform a gap analysis at the functional level. In other words, line managers participate with learning and development in gathering the data required for method-means analysis. And with learning and development's focus on integrated talent management, a shared results chain may be collaboratively created, managed, and evaluated. This practice helps L&D overcome challenges in conducting evaluation by reframing it as an intelligence gathering endeavor with the purpose of organizational learning and improvement. (See appendix B for more information on how to use the L&D Alignment Diagnostic tool and interpret its score.)

Further Recommendations for Improving the Strategic Alignment of L&D

While using the L&D strategic alignment tool generates precise information about where the L&D function should improve its alignment efforts, there are other ways of integrating strategic alignment into your daily business, and, in turn, improving the impact you have on the organization, the customers it serves, and the society to which it contributes. Table 7-3 provides some examples of what these changes might look like.

Table 7-3. Examples of Specific Changes L&D Can Make

Where	Change You May Expect	What That Change May Look Like
Operations	• Skills • Daily work responsibilities • Expectations of self and others • Team responsibilities	• Enhance existing business alignment skills • Replace or modify existing needs assessment processes • Increase business acumen • Replace or modify existing needs assessment processes • Modify current work agreements with internal clients • Adjust the project management schedule to increase time and resources on the front end
Financial	• Allocation of resources and rewards	• Allocate resources based on a documented need • Allocate a smaller percentage of work projects to "have to do" versus "need to do" • Acknowledge and reward strategically aligned projects and participants noting the specific links to outcomes • Apply results from aligned projects in resource allocation decisions
External	• Impact	• Improved value delivered to customers by using relevant data about their needs and priorities • Improved value delivered to employees by using relevant data about their needs and priorities • Improved value delivered to society by using relevant data about the organization's impact, public image, and external trends

Consider the adoption and integration of this process as a way to go about increasing the strategic alignment of your work and also as a continuous effort of transforming the way you and your organization go about selecting and implementing solutions to business problems or opportunities. This is a long-term effort, and you can start with any project you are currently working on or are about to start. You can start with any of these desired changes in your work—a change in individual skills and behaviors, a change in the team's responsibilities or work processes, or a change at the division level that addresses topics such as strategic direction and resource allocation.

That said, many alignment efforts do not start at the corporate level. Instead, you may begin at the division or functional unit level to pilot the alignment efforts. Starting here allows you and stakeholders to gain knowledge, experience, and credibility before extending alignment efforts enterprise-wide. Such an approach sheds light on not only the potential of the performance improvement unit (and its practitioners) to position itself as more strategic and central to the value of the organization, but can also serve as a leader in promoting strategic alignment among and between other units. Such leadership demonstrates an approach to aligning and reinforcing the value being created to a common value proposition. Functional level employees can gain an understanding of how their team and individual efforts contribute to shared goals with employees as owners of capturing strategic value. Thus, the goal of those in performance improvement roles is to facilitate an ongoing synergistic relationship in which learning and development and other business units coordinate their strategies.

Changes in Individual L&D Skills and Behaviors

Using the strategic alignment process may require that you acquire new skills and behaviors, modify existing ones, or eliminate particular skills or behaviors all together. As chapter 1 demonstrated, the roles in training, organization development, and human resource divisions and departments are evolving. And with that, so are the skills and behaviors necessary to carry out transformational work and results. As individuals in the performance improvement profession, you can expect to continuously evolve with the needs of the business and, with that, continuously adapt your skills and behaviors to reflect aligned work, relationships, and results. The following are some ideas for addressing the development of these skills and behaviors:

- **System Thinking Skills**
  - Investigate the system thinking habits of mind and standards.
  - Practice using the system thinking tools in this book.

- ○ Collect data about system thinking behaviors in your organization and track it over time. What does system thinking look like in your organization? In what ways is it being applied? By whom? What are the feedback loops?
- ○ Identify the system thinking tools that are being used in your organization. Which ones could you adopt or modify so they applied to your work?
- ○ Map the structure of your organization. How does this structure influence the behavior within the organization?

- **Strategic Thinking Skills**
  - ○ Design a logic model for your next performance improvement project. This will help develop your thinking in terms of timeframes and their associated, planned consequences. Design for these consequences (that is, outcomes) to the impact level. This will keep your focus on the long-term consequences to customers and society.
  - ○ Follow up with a recent client and ask about the intended and unintended consequences of the project or work. Discuss potential solutions that have produced similar or different results.

- **Critical Thinking Skills**
  - ○ Map the assessment plan for an upcoming project.
  - ○ Design a data collection template for compiling data for a current project.
  - ○ Analyze the data you've compiled for a current project.
  - ○ Discuss your conclusions from a data-driven assessment with colleagues and stakeholders. Incorporate the diverse perspectives.
  - ○ Practice using the root cause analysis tools to dig deeper into the factors that are influencing performance in your organization.

- **Collaboration Skills**
  - ○ Increase the use of face-to-face and telephone communications to redesign your relationships with stakeholders from transactional to transformational.
  - ○ Seek out collaborative opportunities, such as interdepartmental projects.
  - ○ Practice asking new types of questions with your colleagues.
  - ○ Practice negotiating through conflict in work groups; for example, competing approaches to problem solving and decision making.
  - ○ Increase your use of interviews and focus groups, where applicable and aligned, to your methods of data collection.

Changes in L&D Team Responsibilities and Work Processes

Applying the strategic alignment process to your team will require changes to the work products and services they are responsible for delivering and how those work products and services are provided to clients. The work products and services of an aligned performance improvement team are continually changing. This is in response to changing business needs. As the business grows and changes, it is necessary for L&D practitioners, teams, and its division to continuously evolve, and do so at a pace quicker than the business. Performance improvement practitioners, teams, and divisions may then serve as models, coaches, and educators of adapting the products and services they offer and how they go about doing that.

Aligned performance improvement teams apply strategic alignment processes to the majority of their work. However, in reality, not every performance improvement initiative will be informed through the use of documented evidence—some projects just have to be done, but they should occur fewer and farther between. In an aligned state, projects are taken on based on need, rather than order or influence. This requires a strategic plan to be developed in advance, along with work agreements with stakeholders. By doing so, your team is connected to specific strategic initiatives, your resources are communicated, and your influence is directly aligned to strategic outcomes. The aim here is to facilitate the alignment of the majority of the work products produced by your team. The more that are aligned, the more the team will earn a reputation as a valued strategic partner. Some changes that may be considered for the team include:

- Replace or modify existing needs assessment processes.
- Modify current work agreements with internal clients.
- Adjust the project management schedule to increase time and resources on the front end.
- Modify how your team's performance results are communicated.

Changing what work is done and how it is done is a process that will take some time, but the investment will reveal strategically valuable results. It will be well worth the journey. Just as with other performance improvement initiatives, this change in the approach to work on the team should be approached methodically.

The following steps will help you get started:

- Step 1. As a team, complete this sentence: "I will know our team is strategically aligned when . . ." These are your goals.
- Step 2. As a team, determine your desired outcomes—identify what your anticipated results will be at multiple levels.

- Step 3. As a team, determine which strategies will meet your desired outcomes. How will you go about meeting those outcomes?

These first three steps get everyone on the team into a shared agreement about the question, "What are we trying to do?"

- Step 4. As a team, design a long-term assessment plan. Think about how you will collect, analyze, and interpret data that tells you how you are progressing toward your goals.
- Step 5. As a team, negotiate who will take on what role in the assessment plan.
- Step 6. Carry out the assessment plan. Continuously monitor and track your data to gauge how close or far your team is from its desired outcomes.

Steps four through six get everyone on the team to participate in the design and implementation of an assessment plan. This tells the team how well they are doing it.

- Step 7. As a team, share your assessment results with stakeholders. Keep everyone up to date on how the team is progressing toward its goals of facilitating strategic alignment to the business.
- Step 8. With your team and stakeholders, modify and improve the process using the information you've gathered in steps four through six to keep improving. Keep your stakeholders involved in the process. You continue to share in the accountability and the results of your alignment efforts.

These final steps are an opportunity for transparency, shared accountability, and shared results. In these steps, you are keeping your stakeholders involved and informed as your relationship and work changes over time.

Changes at the Divisional Level

When the strategic alignment process is applied at the divisional level of the organization, it influences the processes and identification of the strategic direction and methods for applying resources to performance improvement problems, opportunities, and solutions.

Changes at this level require buy-in and participation from the work groups and teams that fall within the responsibility of the division. Changes to the way work is approached and relationships with stakeholders can represent a fundamental shift for some practitioners, teams, and organizations.

Some changes that may be considered for the division include:

- allocating resources based on documented need
- allocating a smaller percentage of projects to "have to do" versus "should do"
- acknowledging and reward strategically aligned projects and participants noting the specific links to outcomes
- applying results from aligned projects in resource allocation decisions

- modeling the critical skills required of current and future performance improvement practitioners
- mapping the anticipated growth over the next several years and design an assessment plan to monitor and track progress toward those goals.

To facilitate a shared understanding of the new way of going about work, collaboratively consider and negotiate responses to the following questions:

- Why are we doing it? Collaboratively negotiate a shared understanding of the purposes of a strategically aligned workplace, work, and person.
- What guiding principles will we apply to it? Collaboratively negotiate and define shared values that will be applied in a strategically aligned state. How do your values support this endeavor?
- What will be gained from doing it? Collaboratively determine your shared alignment goals. When will you know your division is strategically aligned?
- How do we agree to use it? Collaboratively determine how assessment findings and results will be used. With transparency comes trust. You should agree in advance how the data will—and will not—be used to support these changes.

Conclusion

The work of today's performance improvement practitioners is aimed at creating and leveraging strategic value in organizations. Commonly, organizational leaders will look to the L&D professionals to build employee and organizational capacity so that the organization is positioned to leverage (and capitalize upon) its competitive advantage. This focus on value has been the mantra for the performance improvement profession over the last decades, and with the strategic alignment process, practitioners now have a way to uncover and facilitate that value.

The purpose of a performance improvement practitioner is to develop organizational members to carry out the strategies of the organization. This development comes not only from the lessons learned in the classroom, but also from the lessons derived from performance feedback, which may be leveraged to aid decision making. Supplying timely and accurate performance feedback is the job, and it fulfills the purpose of the performance improvement role. This transformational perspective of today's performance improvement role is purposeful and proactive—it builds upon and grows beyond the traditional, transactional approach to L&D work and interactions with stakeholders. No longer fulfilling training requests ad hoc on a first come, first served basis, according to the products on the shelf, the strategically positioned L&D unit proactively assesses and remedies human performance misalignments between the strategies selected to secure and grow an organization's positioning and capabilities to execute those strategies.

However, the current methods you are using to provide strategic performance feedback may not be answering the right questions. For example, reporting the reactions of participants who attended a customer service class will not tell you what you really want to know: Did the customer service class affect the service performance of course participants? Or, did you realize an increase in sales? Or, are your external customers more satisfied with the service they are receiving? Without connecting the work of the performance improvement role to the business, your ability to inform progress toward your purpose is limited. Like all other functions in the organization, learning and development contributes more than products, yet we favor measuring what we put into a product, the activities we completed for the product, and the product output itself. Imagine evaluating the entire information technology function by the implementation of one system or program. By looking only to the products you have delivered in the past, you miss the opportunity to participate in the formulation of the desired future.

Performance improvement practitioners have much more to offer than products and, as such, require a holistic view of the total, strategically valuable contributions. They offer a quality service to their stakeholders, guiding the selection of L&D choices by using and demonstrating the most pragmatic and timely approach. With effective and efficient outcomes for learning and development and other performance improvement initiatives, everyone wins. While using the strategic alignment process to select learning and development and other performance improvement solutions may be unfamiliar in your organization, remember it is a process. It will take time to recondition the ways in which your organization makes decisions about how to improve performance.

Employers are receptive to viewing performance improvement solutions as strategically valuable; yet, we do not often demonstrate a comprehensive view of the strategic investment of training in organizations or if such investment equates to improvements in firm performance. Performance improvement professionals have an opportunity, especially in cases of progressing from transactional to transformational functions, to proactively influence how and in what ways their work contributes to the strategic priorities of the organization. It is with this perspective and associated effort that L&D professionals may gain their seat at the table and have a part in making the key learning decisions that direct their work and efforts.

A systems approach may be applied to more fully examine the influence of L&D work and its relationship to the firm's performance. This is an opportunity to uncover the unit's influence to measures of organizational growth and productivity, and also measures of employee motivation, turnover, engagement, satisfaction, and so on. Those performance improvement functions that can measurably connect the work they do to the strategic needs of the organization are positioned to demonstrate that their work is strategically valuable. The benefit lies within learning and development's ability to engage in (and foster engagement in) optimized strategic alignment processes. Thus, the alignment activity of performance improvement practitioners is not to strive for the ever allusive (or even unattainable) perfect alignment, but rather to engage in the processes that facilitate ongoing alignment. This offers practitioners a perspective of alignment as an end state and also a dynamic process that reflects ongoing changes in the environment.

Strategic Alignment Process as a Tool for Strategically Valuable Work

The strategic alignment process is a structured, yet flexible, process for ensuring your L&D work is clearly aligned with strategic objectives and generates measurable evidence of your contributions to the organization's success. It aligns your services, products, and programs to business needs, and in turn, business results. This process is conducted collaboratively to generate a shared sense of input and accountability for the work and for the results of that work. This way of doing performance improvement work will shift your view of your current role to that of a performance consultant, architect, and designer. You will begin to see your work and yourself in a different way. Rather than fulfilling training orders using predetermined solutions, you connect the goals of the organization to the solutions you use to achieve those goals. And, you do so collaboratively alongside your stakeholders—sharing in the design, the work, and the results.

New (or further developed) ways of thinking about ourselves and our work are required to apply the strategic alignment process, namely, system thinking, strategic thinking, critical thinking, and collaboration. These skills complement one another throughout the strategic alignment process. Let's take a look at an example. An internal customer in a leadership position noticed that a large number of newer employees were voluntarily leaving the organization within their first year of employment. The leader did not know what the turnover rate should be, but recognized something was off. Why were new hires leaving in such short time?

She asks you to put together a training program for all managers so that they can learn how to hire people who are a better fit for the organization. As the performance improvement professional, you have a couple of options for how to proceed:

- Follow the direction of the requestor and implement the solution she asked for (option 1).
- Engage and negotiate with the requestor to embark on a collaborative performance needs journey (option 2).

The strategic alignment process incorporates these essential skills throughout each stage, which helps performance improvement professionals ensure alignment between the solutions selected to improve performance and the organization's strategic objectives, while also providing a framework for demonstrating the strategic value of L&D work. It enables performance improvement professionals and their respective organizations to look at performance problems and opportunities in a different way, and by doing so derive innovative solutions.

Table 8-1. Comparison of Two Options

Performance Challenge: Last year we experienced a 30% turnover rate of employees with one year or less tenure.	
Option 1	Option 2
• Consider a couple reasons why the turnover happened. • Talk to a handful of others to see what they think is causing the turnover. • Relate to a recent incident as the probable cause. • Design and implement a selection training class for managers. • Conduct a training evaluation to determine if the managers are satisfied with the training class.	• Gather evidence from multiple perspectives (HR, hiring managers, employees). • Identify how the perspectives are related to one another. • Gain commitment from stakeholders to engage in a systems thinking-problem solving approach. • Assess the performance context. • Identify performance success criteria. • Conduct a gap analysis and prioritize the gaps. • Determine the root cause(s) of the high turnover rate. • Identify solution selection criteria. • Select aligned solutions, collaboratively. • Derive long-term implementation, monitoring, and communication plans. • Conduct ongoing and active monitoring of the turnover rate and adjust en route as needs dictate.

The first option is an example of an idea being imposed as the solution—perhaps a habitual response, perhaps we don't want to "turn work away"—it's what our customer is used to. A stakeholder begins with an idea in mind, such as an L&D solution, and directs the HR-related team to implement it. A problem or challenge may have prompted the idea, but a search for the solution is not performed. Measurable targets that show success (or nonsuccess) of the solution are not set. The stakeholder gains credibility and buy-in for the decision by securing the acceptance of others, often key decision makers, who deem it valuable and thus assume that this will lead to employees adopting the solution and positive outcomes. Those who take this idea imposition approach often do so because these behaviors are assumed to be timely and pragmatic—quick decisions and immediate action are rewarded.

The second option is geared toward discovery. In this case, decision makers start with a focus on performance, rather than solution. They gather support for the performance problem to show that the problem is real—there is an issue of performance that requires our attention. Rather than presenting a specific solution next, discovery decision makers enlist others in the search for a solution and use targets to guide the efforts. This process communicates that improvement in performance is both desirable and feasible, while at the same time gains momentum for early and sustainable adoption for the solution. A solution is then selected and once implemented, receives ongoing monitoring to verify the solution is meeting the performance need. This approach is not as popular as idea imposition as it is regarded as taking too much time, and therefore, is more expensive. It is also assumed that it is not realistic for today's organizational decision making.

So, in a world that demands quick action and decision making, how does a performance improvement practitioner apply a discovery approach tool, such as the strategic alignment process, successfully?

Researchers have looked into not only what the process of decision making in organizations looks like, but also what the outcomes of each approach are likely to be. In other words, which approach is more successful? Table 8-2 shows their findings.

Table 8-2. Comparison of Two Decision-Making Approaches

Approach	Implementation Rate	Average Time to Perform	Success in Meeting Outcome Goal	Adoption and Sustainability Rate
Idea Imposition	51%	20.5 months	41-55%	41-55%
Discovery	72%	11.9 months	90-100%	85-90%

Adapted from Nutt (2008).

Surprising? While we may have guessed that a discovery approach would produce better outcomes, what may be surprising is that it actually takes less time, that solutions born from this approach have a much better chance of being adopted and sustained by employees, and that more of these types of decisions actually get the green light to move forward.

Making the Transition to a Strategic Alignment Approach

Your stakeholders may be accustomed to reaching out to the L&D professionals to impose a solution, such as a training program, as their go-to solution, so altering the ways in which you respond to such requests will be important. This is your opportunity to begin changing the paradigm about what products and services you and your team can offer to support performance in the organization. While the way you conduct business may be different from what your stakeholders are used to experiencing, don't let this stop you from breaking with tradition. You are establishing a partnership with the requestor. In time, you and your stakeholders will have a closer consultative relationship focused on strategic decision making that delivers performance results, rather than a strictly transactional relationship focused solely on the delivery of a learning service or product.

To test it out, try using this approach on one of your stakeholders whom you anticipate being most amenable to a change in the way you interact when making L&D choices. Find an early adopter and keep progressing. As you achieve success, others will take notice that your approach produces better outcomes, is timelier, pragmatic, and it's not just another L&D fad.

L&D solutions can be expensive endeavors for organizations, so it's critical to consider how we go about making good decisions for what L&D solutions to invest in. Those in HR-related roles, such as talent development, talent management, and organization development, can help their stakeholders make decisions about L&D strategies using criteria that's important to them—timely implementation, strategies with the greatest chance of being adopted by employees, and those that will offer a positive return for the investment. Are you ready to get started?

Appendix A

Strategic Alignment Process Toolbox

Each chapter contained tools to guide your progress. Modify and adjust these tools as you see fit and for what is most appropriate given the performance context.

ALIGN Expectations

Use This Tool	If You Would Like to	Pg.
Stakeholder Table	Identify relevant stakeholders for your project	129
Stakeholder Mapping Tool	Assess the influence and importance of your stakeholders' thoughts and definitions of successful project outcomes	130
Discovery Meeting Focus Areas and Sample Questions	Gain information that deepens your understanding of the issues and factors that may affect successful project outcomes	131
Strategic Skills, Behaviors, and Attributes That Support Partnerships With Clients Checklist	Assess various perspectives of your business acumen, personal attributes, and technical skills	132
Calibration Matrix	Map and weight stakeholder perspectives of the problem or opportunity, understanding of context, and level of partnership and commitment to the project	133
Information Credibility of Stakeholder Expectations Worksheet	Assess the relevancy, reliability, validity, and thoroughness of stakeholder performance expectations	134
Alignment Mapping Tool	Map the various stakeholder perspectives according to alignment level	135
ALIGN Expectations Checklist	Assess various perspectives of your aligning expectations performance	136

ALIGN Results

Use This Tool	If You Would Like to	Pg.
Results and Gaps Template	To compare results and gaps in those results	137
Logic Model	Depict the relationships between organizational goals, strategic priorities, and stakeholder expectations	138
Sample Indicators Grouped by Level of Results	Identify relevant data at each level	139
Data Collection Strategy Template	Collaboratively design a data collection strategy with stakeholders	140
ALIGN Results Checklist	Assess perspectives of your aligning results performance	141

ALIGN Solutions

Use This Tool	If You Would Like to	Pg.
Align Gaps to Level of Results Table	Align gaps to each level of result	142
Gap Selection Criteria Rubric	Identify gap selection decision-making criteria of stakeholders	143
Gap Decision Criteria Scoring Worksheet	Assess gap selection decision making criteria of stakeholders	144
Root Cause Analysis Template	Analyze root causes of performance	145
Force Field Analysis Worksheet	Analyze drivers and barriers to performance within and outside your organization	146
Solution Selection Decision Criteria Checklist	Identify solution decision making criteria of stakeholders	147
Solution Decision Criteria Scoring Worksheet	Assess solution decision making criteria of stakeholders	148
Sample Environmental and Individual Performance Solutions Table	Create solutions specific to environmental or individual factors	149
Solution Options Rubric	Collaboratively select aligned solutions with stakeholders	150
Selected Environmental and Individual Solutions Template	Negotiate solution options with stakeholders	151
ALIGN Solutions Checklist	Assess various perspectives of your aligning solutions performance	152

ALIGN Implementation

Use This Tool	If You Would Like to	Pg.
Sample Transfer Strategy Considerations Table	Identify change management strategies	153
Timing and Sample Transfer Strategies Table	Derive thoughtful change management strategies to facilitate integration of your performance improvement work	154
Performance Measures for Each Alignment Level	Design a monitoring plan to ensure regular performance feedback	155
Sample Communication Planner	Design strategies that promote ongoing collaboration and shared accountability with your stakeholders	156
ALIGN Implementation Checklist	Assess various perspectives of your aligning implementation performance	157

ALIGN Expectations

Tool: Stakeholder Table

Purpose: Identify relevant stakeholders for your project.

Relevant Stakeholders	
What is the initial problem?	
Which individuals or groups may affect or be affected by this project?	
Who are the influential change agents? Describe their possible impact.	
Which individuals or groups may offer resistance to change? Why?	
What are potential barriers to adoption?	

Tool: Stakeholder Mapping Tool

Purpose: Assess the influence and importance of your various stakeholders' decisions and assumptions and their definitions of successful project outcomes.

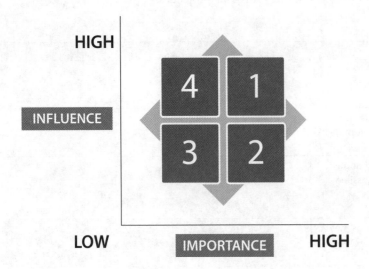

Each quadrant can be analyzed in the following way, in a clockwise rotation:

- **Quadrant one:** Stakeholders placed here have high influence and high importance (for example, leadership, key managers, or supervisors) need to be fully engaged on the strategic alignment process. The style of participation for stakeholders needs to be appropriate for gaining and maintaining their ownership.

- **Quadrant two:** Stakeholders placed here can be highly important but having low influence or direct power (for example, employees directly affected by the potential learning or performance improvement program), however need to be kept informed through appropriate education and communication.

- **Quadrant three:** Stakeholders here have low influence and low importance, however, should still be monitored and kept on board, as their relative position could change at any time. For example, these individuals could switch roles, and with that there may be an increase in their influence within the organization, as well as a potential for greater decision-making authority over resources.

- **Quadrant four:** Stakeholders placed here can have potentially high influence but low importance (or relevance) to the potential performance improvement efforts. They should be kept satisfied with appropriate approval and perhaps brought in as patrons or supporters who "endorse" the strategic alignment process of the potential performance improvement program.

Tool: Discovery Meeting Focus Areas and Sample Questions

Purpose: Gain information that deepens your understanding of the issues and factors that may affect successful project outcomes.

Area of Focus	Sample Questions I Can Ask
Perceived performance challenge or opportunity	• What brought the requestor to seek help? • What is being requested (for example, a predetermined • solution or help in problem solving)? • How important is this problem or opportunity? • Who is currently being impacted, and/or whom will it impact? How? • Who may impact it? How? • What evidence has led each stakeholder to his or her conclusions?
Solution context and organizational environment	• If a specific solution is being requested, in what ways will the solution be supported in the current work environment? • In what ways may the current work environment impede the solution? • What type of management support (for example, allocation of resources) exists for the solution(s)?
Expectations of performance	• What does performance look like today? • What results (or outputs) are currently being accomplished? • What should performance look like after the solution is implemented? • What tangible results should be delivered by performers? • What criteria will be used to determine whether these results are satisfactory? • Who will determine/judge whether the results obtained are satisfactory based on these criteria? • What, if any, evidence suggests that employees are clear about the performance expectation? • What if any gaps exists between desired and current results.
Connections to organizational objectives	• To what business objective(s) does the performance issue relate? How? • What business goal(s) will our selected solution affect? How and to what extent? • What skills are required to fulfill the performance objective? • In addition to skills, what else (for example, resources, support) may be required to fulfill the performance objective?
Partnership and collaboration items	• What is the best way to collaborate with/support you? • What other partnerships are critical to the success of our solution(s)? • How do we ensure these partnerships are effective? • Describe the process of collaborating with your stakeholders (what they can expect from you, what you can expect from them throughout the life cycle of the solution)? • What barriers or challenges might you/we encounter? • How can we overcome these challenges?

Tool: Strategic Skills, Behaviors, and Attributes That Support Partnerships With Clients Checklist

Purpose: Assess various perspectives of your business acumen, personal attributes, and technical skills.

Skill, Behavior, or Attribute	Examples	Check
Your business acumen	You have an understanding of the emerging needs of the business	
	You know the business value chain	
	You communicate in business language (written and verbal)	
	You have an understanding of the context in which the business operates	
	You are deeply aware of what is necessary to execute the organization's strategies (short and long term)	
	You have an understanding of how your efforts are linked to the organization's mission	
Your personal attributes	Your teamwork approach to problem solving and decision making	
	Your communication skills (good listener, probing for more information, confidence in speaking with all audience levels)	
	You work proactively and continuously to develop and foster trust (ethical, integrity)	
	You are sincere in your desire to create win-win outcomes for those who will affect and be affected by the solution	
	You are responsive to business and personal needs and can balance these appropriately	
	You are transparent with your work	
	You work proactively to gain support from management	
Your technical skills	You provide the business case for all learning decisions	
	You plan how learning interventions will be integrated throughout the organization	
	You conduct gap analysis to inform the design and delivery of strategic interventions	
	You offer just in time learning solutions to address current business needs	

Tool: Calibration Matrix

Purpose: Map and weight the various stakeholder perspectives of the performance problem or opportunity, understanding of the performance context, and level of partnership and commitment to the project.

Stakeholder	Performance Problem or Opportunity		Performance Context			Alignment to Organizational Objectives	Partnership and Commitment		
	Perceived problem or opportunity	Performance expectations	Culture	Supports	Barriers	Organizational objective(s) being addressed	Resistance level	Solution openness level	Overall commitment level
Stakeholder 1							H M L	H M L	H M L
Stakeholder 2							H M L	H M L	H M L
Stakeholder 3							H M L	H M L	H M L
							H M L	H M L	H M L
							H M L	H M L	H M L

Tool: Information Credibility of Stakeholder Expectations Worksheet

Purpose: Assess the relevancy, reliability, validity, and thoroughness of stakeholder performance expectations.

Stakeholder	Performance Expectations			
	Relevant	Reliable	Valid	Thorough
Stakeholder 1				
Stakeholder 2				
Stakeholder 3				

Tool: Alignment Mapping Tool

Purpose: Map stakeholder expectations to alignment level.

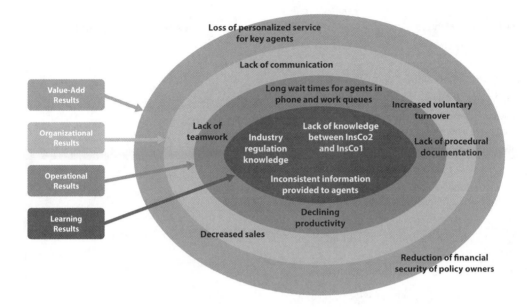

Tool: ALIGN Expectations Checklist

Purpose: Assess various perspectives of your aligning expectations performance.

Element of Alignment	Yes/No	How To
My System Thinking		
I have carefully thought through the context of the performance challenge or opportunity	Y/N	
My Strategic Thinking		
I have performed an objective analysis by investigating: what, when, why, where, and how	Y/N	
My Critical Thinking		
I recognize that a problem (or opportunity) exists	Y/N	
I have developed an orderly approach in which tasks are organized and problems are recognized based on severity and urgency	Y/N	
I have synthesized information from a variety of sources	Y/N	
I have determined the credibility of the information provided by my stakeholders	Y/N	
I asked the right questions of my stakeholders	Y/N	
My Collaboration With Stakeholders		
I have developed an openness to a variety of perspectives	Y/N	
I have encouraged my stakeholders to develop an openness to a variety of perspectives	Y/N	
I have used effective listening skills to better understand the expectations of my stakeholders	Y/N	
I have communicated my support of teamwork and shared accountability for the performance problem or opportunity	Y/N	
I have used business language with my stakeholders to communicate my understanding of the performance problem or opportunity	Y/N	
I have used business language to communicate the value in creating alignment	Y/N	
Is this the right partner/project to try out a new process for responding to talent development and management requests?	Y/N	

ALIGN Results

Tool: Results and Gaps Template

Purpose: To compare results and gaps in those results.

Results	Indicators	Target	Current	Gap
Desired results of the stake-holders and organization	Data we'll track to measure progress	Where we'd like to be	Where we are today	The difference between
Value-Add Results				
Organizational Results				
Operational Results				
Learning Results				

Tool: Logic Model

Purpose: Depict the relationships between organizational goals, strategic priorities, and stakeholder expectations.

Our Planned Work		The Shared Results of Our Work		
Activities	Outputs	Operational Results	Organizational Results	Value-Add Results
What we do	What we produce	The raw results we affect	The progress we affect	The change we affect

Tool: Sample Indicators Grouped by Level of Results

Purpose: Identify relevant data at each level.

Level	Required Results	Sample Indicator(s)
Value-Add		
Organizational		
Operational		
Learning		

Tool: Data Collection Strategy Template

Purpose: Collaboratively design a data collection strategy with stakeholders.

Results	Indicators	Sources	Methods	Data Analysis
The desired results of my stakeholders and organization	The data we'll track to measure progress	Who and where we will get the data from; Sampling techniques	How we will get the data; How often it will be collected	How we will analyze the data to make sense of it: When this will be done; How often
Value-Add Results				
Organizational Results				
Operational Results				
Learning Results				

Tool: ALIGN Results Checklist

Purpose: Assess various perspectives of your aligning results performance.

Element of Alignment	Yes/No	How To
My Strategic Thinking		
I identified gaps between where the organization is today and where it wants to be in the future	Y/N	
I have assessed the performance context	Y/N	
My Critical Thinking		
I have identified gaps between where the organization is today and where we want to be in the future	Y/N	
I synthesized information from a variety of sources	Y/N	
I determined the credibility of the information I gathered from all relevant sources	Y/N	
I have carefully synthesized the data to identify the appropriate alignment level	Y/N	
I used existing information where possible to avoid duplication when I collected data	Y/N	
My Collaboration With Stakeholders		
I presented coherent and persuasive arguments for controversial or difficult issues	Y/N	
I used my effective listening skills to better understand value from the perspectives of my stakeholders	Y/N	
I collaborated with stakeholders to identify the critical success criteria and measurable indicators for performance improvements	Y/N	
I drove teamwork by recognizing and rewarding the achievement of goals, rather than individual performance	Y/N	
I established partnerships and reduced silo work by teaming up with other groups in the organization	Y/N	
I supported and committed to group decisions that fostered teamwork and shared accountability for our efforts	Y/N	

ALIGN Solutions

Tool: Align Gaps to Level of Results Table

Purpose: Align gaps to each level of result.

Level of Results	Identified Gaps
Value-Add	
Organizational	
Operational	
Learning	

Tool: Gap Selection Criteria Rubric

Purpose: Identify gap selection decision-making criteria of stakeholders.

Gap Selection Criteria	Description and Considerations	Stakeholder Rating (3 = High; 1 = Low)		
		S. 1	S. 2	S. 3
Priority	• High—Must address now • Medium—May address in near future, add to a future phase, or postpone • Low—Can ignore			
Scope involved in closing the gap	• Activities and tasks required to do the work • Resources required to do the work • Deliverables the project will (and will not) produce • Anticipated constraints in addressing the gap • Assumptions related to addressing the gap			
Importance of closing the gap to others	• High—It's important to others that we address the gap • Moderate—It's somewhat important to others, or important to some of our stakeholders • Low—It's not very important to others			
Anticipated consequences	• What are the potential consequences of addressing and not addressing the gap?			
Magnitude	• What is the reach of the gap?			
Costs	• High-level financial estimates of closing and not closing it • High-level nonfinancial estimates of closing and not closing it			
Other alignment levels	• How would closing the gap affect other alignment levels? Other gaps? • How would not closing the gap affect other alignment levels? Other gaps?			
Resources	• What resources are required to close the gap? • What resources would be consumed by not closing it?			

Tool: Gap Decision Criteria Scoring Worksheet

Purpose: Assess gap selection decision-making criteria of stakeholders.

Scorer Name	Priority	Scope	Importance	Consequences	Magnitude	Costs	Levels	Resources
S. 1								
S. 2								
S. 3								
Total by selection area								

Tool: Root Cause Analysis Template

Purpose: Analyze root causes of performance.

	Information	Resources	Incentives
Environmental Factors That Influence Performance			

	Knowledge and Skills	Capacity	Motives
Individual Factors That Influence Performance			

Tool: Force Field Analysis Worksheet

Purpose: Analyze drivers and barriers to performance within and outside your organization.

Driving Force (positive)	Force Strength											Restraining Force (negative)
	+5	+4	+3	+2	+1	0	-1	-2	-3	-4	-5	

Adapted from Chevalier (2003).

Tool: Solution Selection Decision Criteria Checklist

Purpose: Identify solution decision-making criteria of stakeholders.

Criterion	Defined	Scoring
Probability	What is the probability that this solution will close the gap?	3-High probability 2-Moderate probability 1-Low probability 0-No probability
Appropriateness	Does this solution make sense for our business, culture, and environment?	3-Very appropriate 2-Moderately appropriate 1-Somewhat appropriate 0-Not at all appropriate
Ability to support	What is the organizational ability to support the solution long term?	3-High ability 2-Moderate ability 1-Low ability 0-No ability
Barriers and constraints	What are the organizational barriers or constraints to implementing the solution long term?	3-No barriers or constraints 2-Low barriers or constraints 1-Moderate barriers or constraints 0-High barriers or constraints
Acceptability	What is the anticipated acceptance of those who will affect or be affected by the solution long term?	3-High acceptance 2-Moderate acceptance 1-Low acceptance 0-No acceptance
Time to implement	What is the anticipated total time required to implement the solution?	3-Time is not a concern 2-Time to implement is reasonable 1-Time to implement is a stretch but manageable 0-Time to implement is unreasonable
Cost to implement	What are the total costs of the solution (effort, time away from current work, maintenance)?	3-Below budget 2-Reasonable and within budget 1-A stretch, but manageable 0-Unreasonable, not doable

Tool: Solution Decision Criteria Scoring Worksheet

Purpose: Assess solution decision-making criteria of stakeholders.

Scorer Name	Probability	Appropriateness	Ability to Support	Barriers and Constraints	Acceptance	Time	Cost
Total by Decision Criteria							

Tool: Sample Environmental and Individual Performance Solutions Table

Purpose: Sample solutions specific to environmental or individual factors.

	Information	Resources	Incentives
Environmental Performance Solutions	• Documented performance standards (e.g., standard operating procedures) • Content management system • Performance feedback (formal and informal) • Information sharing system • Reduce silo work • Redesign workflows	• Supply necessary tools and equipment • Provide necessary time to perform as expected • Provide access to people and networks	• Identify employee performance goals • Align employee and organizational performance goals • Realign rewards to desired performance outcomes • Recognize superior performance
	Knowledge and Skills	**Capacity**	**Motives**
Individual Performance Solutions	• On-the-job or classroom training • Role play • Self-study	• Establish job and competency profiles • Establish selection protocol with performance-based measures • Create performance-based assessments for positions • Perform realistic job previews	• Identify and facilitate line of sight between employee work and organizational goals • Identify individual incentives • Eliminate or reduce barriers to performance

Tool: Solution Options Rubric

Purpose: Collaboratively assess multiple solution options with stakeholders.

	Solution 1	Solution 2	Solution 3
Probability			
Ability to Support			
Cost to Implement			
Appropriateness			
Barriers and Constraints			
Acceptability			
Time to Implement			
Chance of Success			

Tool: Selected Environmental and Individual Solutions Template

Purpose: Negotiate solution options with stakeholders.

	Information	Resources	Incentives
Environmental Performance Solutions			

	Knowledge and Skills	Capacity	Motives
Individual Performance Solutions			

Tool: ALIGN Solutions Checklist

Purpose: Assess various perspectives of your aligning solutions performance.

Element of Alignment	Yes/No	How To
My System Thinking		
I outlined relationships and consequences for the various solutions	Y/N	
My Strategic Thinking		
I recommended appropriately aligned improvements to help the organization realize our desired results	Y/N	
I planned ahead by anticipating multiple scenarios and appropriate courses of action	Y/N	
My Critical Thinking		
I generated a reasoned method for selecting among several solution options	Y/N	
I applied metacognitive knowledge so that I could monitor my own performance	Y/N	
My Collaboration With Stakeholders		
I have communicated a commitment to foster teamwork and shared accountability for group decision making about the performance solution	Y/N	
I facilitated an openness to a variety of solutions	Y/N	
I presented coherent and persuasive arguments for controversial or difficult issues	Y/N	
I drove teamwork by recognizing and rewarding the achievement of goals, rather than individual performance	Y/N	
I established partnerships and reduced silo work by teaming up with other groups in the organization	Y/N	
I supported and committed to group decisions that fostered teamwork and shared accountability for our efforts	Y/N	

ALIGN Implementation

Tool: Sample Transfer Strategy Considerations Table

Purpose: Identify change management strategies.

Transfer Considerations	Transfer Strategies
How will the solution be used on the job?	
How will the solution be supported on the job?	
What are the anticipated supports and barriers of the solution being used on the job?	
What are the employees' opportunities to use and integrate the solution on the job?	
Who are the SMEs for this solution, if applicable?	
What is the plan for the design of the solution?	
What is the deployment plan for the solution?	
How often will you follow up with stakeholders after the solution is implemented?	
How will you follow up with those who are using the solution on the job? How will you monitor its progress?	
How and when will you communicate progress with stakeholders?	
What tasks are required to implement the solution?	
How will you cascade the solutions?	

Tool: Timing and Sample Transfer Strategies Table

Purpose: Derive thoughtful change management strategies to facilitate integration of your performance improvement work.

When to Use Transfer Strategy	Transfer Strategy Tasks and Activities
Before Implementation	
During Implementation	
After Implementation	

Tool: Performance Measures for Each Alignment Level

Purpose: Design a monitoring plan to ensure regular performance feedback.

Alignment Level	Result	Performance Measures
Value-Add	Aligning solutions to the needs of external clients, society, or the community	
Organizational	Aligning solutions to the organization's bottom line	
Operational	Aligning solutions with specific accomplishments of a person or a group	
Learning	Aligning solutions with how work is done	

Tool: Sample Communication Planner

Purpose: Design strategies that promote ongoing collaboration and shared accountability with your stakeholders.

Communication Owner	What Is Being Communicated	Why It Is Being Communicated	Who Receives the Communication	When and How It Is Communicated

Tool: ALIGN Implementation Checklist

Purpose: Assess various perspectives of your aligning implementation performance.

Element of Alignment	Yes/No	How To
My System Thinking		
I am able to make sense of how the change will influence performance at multiple levels in the organization	Y/N	
I am able to determine what will help desired performance happen	Y/N	
I was able to determine what may get in the way of desired performance	Y/N	
My Strategic Thinking		
I did an objective analysis by investigating what, when, why, where, and how	Y/N	
I thought about how the people, processes, and structures will change	Y/N	
My Critical Thinking		
I recommended strategies for use of the solution on the job	Y/N	
Collaboratively, a monitoring plan was developed to track the solution	Y/N	
I explored the short-term and long-term outcomes of the solution	Y/N	
I am able to forecast the impact of the solution	Y/N	
My Collaboration With Stakeholders		
I presented coherent and persuasive arguments for controversial or difficult issues	Y/N	
I used my effective listening skills to better understand value from the perspectives of my stakeholders	Y/N	
I established partnerships and reduced silo work by teaming up with other groups in the organization	Y/N	
I supported and committed to group decisions that fostered teamwork and shared accountability for our efforts	Y/N	
I negotiated the next course of action with my stakeholders	Y/N	

Appendix B

L&D Alignment Diagnostic

The proactive charge of the L&D function is to drive and develop performance within. To fulfill this charge, we provide a diagnostic tool to determine the level of alignment of the L&D function.

L&D Alignment Diagnostic

Item	Strongly Disagree	Disagree	Somewhat Agree	Agree	Strongly Agree
1. L&D understands the emerging needs of the business	1	2	3	4	5
2. L&D knows the business value chain	1	2	3	4	5
3. L&D has confidence to speak in business terms to line executives	1	2	3	4	5
4. L&D strategic execution plans are communicated in business language	1	2	3	4	5
5. L&D understands the context in which the business operates	1	2	3	4	5
6. L&D is deeply aware of what is necessary to execute a firm's strategies	1	2	3	4	5
7. L&D understands how its efforts are linked to the organization's mission	1	2	3	4	5
8. L&D provides ongoing communication of the business case for solutions or initiatives	1	2	3	4	5
9. The L&D function works proactively with line managers to develop trust	1	2	3	4	5
10. There is an internal climate of cooperation where the learning function can exercise its role in creating strategic alignment	1	2	3	4	5
11. L&D receives support from line managers	1	2	3	4	5
12. The L&D function plans how interventions will be integrated throughout the organization.	1	2	3	4	5
13. Just-in-time learning solutions are offered to address current business needs	1	2	3	4	5
14. The learning function has ongoing dialogue with line managers	1	2	3	4	5
15. Gap analysis is performed to inform the design and delivery of strategic interventions	1	2	3	4	5

This diagnostic questionnaire lists the L&D skills and behaviors identified as most critical to the strategic alignment and contributions of L&D and has been validated by some 500 L&D practitioners and experts with a wide range of expertise and levels of experience. You may choose to use this questionnaire to conduct a self-assessment of your ongoing progress in improving the strategic alignment of your work. You may also choose to give this questionnaire to your stakeholders to assess improvements in stakeholders' perceptions of the strategic alignment of your work.

How to Use the Tool

The tool can be administered to internal and external L&D stakeholders. Specifically, you can use it to gain an understanding of L&D members' own perceptions of strategic alignment, as well as to organizational members, whom the L&D function supports. This perception of alignment matters, as it can have an impact on commitment to and sustainability of L&D efforts. Therefore, this tool is meant to provide you with data on the perceptions of strategic alignment, which you can use to clearly measure gaps between desired versus current levels of strategic alignment and allow you to identify gaps.

The items that reveal the biggest gaps could be used to trigger an analysis of the barriers to higher scores, and in turn, to select specific actions to help improve those scores. For example, if particularly low scores are observed in "Gap analysis is performed to inform the design and delivery of strategic interventions," you can initiate an analysis that helps you determine why the L&D team is not carrying out (or being perceived as not carrying out) gap analyses. You might find that this expectation has not been clearly communicated to L&D team members or linked to their performance evaluations. You may find that they don't know how to conduct a performance-based gap analysis, because their education and experience has been limited to an instructional or training-based gap analysis, or they simply may not have the confidence to engage in such a process with line managers.

Whatever the barriers, they will inform what actions you should take to enhance L&D's contributions in those areas. The tool would be administered periodically (perhaps annually) to determine trends in the strategic alignment of the L&D function, somewhat similar to an annual strategic alignment score card.

The tool could also be adapted to serve as the basis for recruiting, hiring, and developing L&D staff. The L&D function is undergoing a paradigm shift from providing preferred or familiar learning solutions to delivering measurable results that contribute to the organization's strategic objectives. This requires an expanded focus for L&D professionals who must have expertise and experience with more than learning sciences, methods and technologies. They must now also competently apply a broad range of improvement sciences and practices in the pursuit of supporting the execution of strategic objectives.

Scoring and Interpretation

One simple logic for scoring the results of the tool is to assign the point value illustrated for each response option (1-5). That is, each item could be scored at a maximum of 5 points, and a minimum of 1 point. Based on the maximum possible points per item, an ideal scenario would be for the total L&D Strategic Alignment score to be 75 (5 point x 15 items). The target score you choose for your L&D function may be lower than that, and ultimately, your L&D leadership, with input from others, will have the responsibility for setting the targets.

Your gaps would then be estimated by comparing the actual average score to the ideal score, in which your actual average is calculated by estimating the average score earned from the group of respondents.

Target	Actual (average group score)	Gap
75	62	13 pts

It may also be useful to differentiate your average score between two groups: internal L&D team, on the one hand, and the other functions L&D serves, on the other. Understanding the differences between the perceptions of these groups could help identify miscommunication and missed expectations. For example, the L&D team may think it is operating strategically, but its clients may as a group have a much lower perception of their strategic alignment and contributions.

Target	Average External Group Score	Average Internal (L&D) score
75	62	73

The same logic could be used to understand how well you are meeting the strategic execution needs of various organizational functions, divisions, and geographic locations.

Function	Target	Actual Group Score
Legal Compliance	75	
Research and Development	75	64
Sales	75	69
Assembly	75	45
Marketing and Communications	75	56

There are many categories you could use to drill down on the data and understand the specific perceptions of stakeholder groups. Your L&D function should discuss and determine your particular decision-making needs, which will inform how you want to disaggregate the data.

References and Related Readings

Aguinis, H. 2007. *Performance Management.* Upper Saddle River, NJ: Pearson.

Aguinis, H., H. Joo, and R.K. Gottfredson 2011. "Why We Hate Performance Management and Why We Should Love It." *Business Horizons* 54: 503-507. doi:10.1016/j.bushor.2011.06.001.

Anderson, V. 2008. "A View From the Top: Executive Perceptions of the Value of Learning." *Strategic HR Review* 7(4): 11-16.

ASTD (American Society for Training & Development). 2009. T*he Value of Evaluation: Making Training Evaluations More Effective.* ASTD Press: Alexandria, VA.

ASTD (American Society for Training & Development). 2011. *State of the Industry.* Alexandria, VA: ASTD Press.

Baldwin, T.T., 2009. "Transfer of Training 1988-2008: An Updated Review and New Agenda for Future Research." In G.P. Hodgkinson and J.K. Ford (eds.), *International Review of Industrial and Organizational Psychology* 24: 41-70. Chichester, UK: Wiley.

Baldwin, T.T., and J.K. Ford. 1988. "Transfer of Training: A Review and Directions for Future Research." *Personnel Psychology* 41(1): 63-105.

Barrett, A., and P.J. O'Connell. 2000. "Does Training Generally Work: The Returns to In-Company Training." *Industrial & Labor Relations Review* 54(3): 647-662.

Beer, M. 1980. *Organization Change and Development: A Systems View.* Santa Monica, CA: Goodyear.

Beer, M., and R.A. Eisenstat. 1996. "Developing an Organization Capable of Implementing Strategy and Learning." *Human Relations* 49(5): 597–619.

Beer, M., R.A. Eisenstat, and B. Spector. 1990. *The Critical Path to Corporate Renewal.* Boston: Harvard Business School Press.

Berger, W. 2016. *A More Beautiful Question: The Power of Inquiry to Spark Breakthrough Ideas.* New York: Bloomsbury.

Berson, Y., and B. Avolio. 2004. "Transformational Leadership and the Dissemination of Organizational Goals: A Case Study of a Telecommunication Firm." *Leadership Quarterly* 15: 625–646.

Bird, A. and S. Beechler. 1995. "Links Between Business Strategy and Human Resource Management Strategy in U.S.-Based Japanese Subsidiaries: An Empirical Investigation." *Journal of International Business Studies* 26(1): 23-46.

Biron, M., E. Farndale, and J. Paauwe. 2011. "Performance Management Effectiveness: Lessons From World-Leading Firms." *The International Journal of Human Resource Management* 22: 1294-1311. doi:10.1080/09585192.2011.559100.

Bommer, W.H., G.A. Rich, and R.S. Rubin. 2005. "Changing Attitudes About Change: Longitudinal Effects of Transformational Leader Behavior on Employee Cynicism About Organizational Change." *Journal of Organizational Behavior* 26: 733–753.

Brethower, D. 2009. "It Isn't Magic, It's Science." *Performance Improvement Quarterly* 48(10): 18-24.

Burke, L.A., and H.M. Hutchins. 2008. "A Study of Best Practices in Training Transfer and Proposed Model of Transfer." *Human Resource Development Quarterly* 19: 107–28.

Burke, W., and G. Litwin. 1992. "A Causal Model Of Organizational Performance and Change." *Journal of Management* 18: 523–545.

Chan, Y.E., S.L. Huff, D.W. Barclay, and D.G. Copeland. 1997. "Business Strategic Orientation, Information Systems Strategic Orientation, and Strategic Alignment." *Information Systems Research* 8(2): 125-150.

Chevalier, R. 2003. "Updating the Behavioral Engineering Model." *Performance Improvement Quarterly* 42(5): 8-14.

Christiansen, L.C., and M. Higgs. 2008. "How the Alignment of Business Strategy and HR Strategy Can Impact Performance." *Journal of General Management* 33(4): 13-33.

Clark, R.E., and F. Estes 2000. *Turning Research Into Results: A Guide to Selecting the Right Performance Solutions.* Atlanta: CEP Press.

Craft, A., H. Gardner, and C. Claxton. 2015. "Nurturing Creativity, Wisdom, and Trusteeship in Education." In K. Chappell, T. Cremin, and B. Jeffrey (eds.). *Creativity, Education and Society: Writings of Anna Craft.* London: Institute of Education Press, 143-157.

Eisenhardt, K. 1998. "Decision Making and All That Jazz." In V. Papadakis and P. Barwise (eds.), *Strategic Decisions.* Norwell, MA: Kluwer.

Fitzgerald, L., R. Johnston, and S. Brignall. 1991. *Performance Measurement in Service Businesses.* London: CIMA Publishing.

Ford, J.K., S.L. Yelon, and A.Q. Billington. 2011. "How Much Is Transferred From Training to the Job? The 10% Delusion as a Catalyst for Thinking About Transfer." *Performance Improvement Quarterly* 24(2): 7-24.

Gilbert, T. 1978. "The Behavior Engineering Model." In *Human Competence: Engineering Worthy Performance,* 73-105. New York: McGraw-Hill.

Gilley, J.W., A. Maycunich, and S.A. Quatro. 2002. "Comparing the Roles, Responsibilities, and Activities of Transactional and Transformational HRD Professionals." *Performance Improvement Quarterly* 15(4): 23-44.

Gruman, J.A., and A.M. Saks. 2011. "Performance Management and Employee Engagement." *Human Resource Management Review* 21(2): 123-136.

Guerra-López, I. 2008 *Performance Evaluation: Proven Approaches for Improving Program and Organizational Performance.* San Francisco: Jossey-Bass.

Guerra, López, I. 2013. "Performance Indicator Maps: A Visual Tool for Understanding, Managing, and Continuously Improving Your Business Metrics." *Performance Improvement Journal.*

Guerra-López, I. 2014. "Organizational Learning and Performance." In M. Spector (ed.), *Encyclopedia for Educational Technology.* Thousand Oaks, CA: Sage Publishing.

Guerra-López, I., and K. Hicks. 2015a. "The Participatory Design and Implementation of a Monitoring and Evaluation System in an International Development Environment." *Evaluation and Program Planning.* 48: 21-39.

Guerra-López, I., and K. Hicks. 2015b. "Turning Trainers into Strategic Business Partners." *TD at Work.* Alexandria, VA. ATD Press.

Guerra-López, I., and A. Hutchinson. 2013. "Measurable and Continuous Performance Improvement: The Development of a Performance Measurement, Management, and Improvement System." *Performance Improvement Quarterly* 26(2).

Guerra-López, I., and M. Norris-Thomas. 2011. "Making Sound Decisions: A Framework for Judging the Worth of Your Data." *Performance Improvement Journal* 50(5): 37-44.

Hicks, K. 2016. "Construct Validation of Strategic Alignment in Learning and Talent Development." *Performance Improvement Quarterly* 28(4): 71-89.

Hammond, J.S., R.L. Keeney, and H. Raiffan. 1998. "The Hidden Traps in Decision Making." *Harvard Business Review,* September-October.

Hicks, K 2016. "Construct Validation of Strategic Alignment in Learning and Talent Development." *Performance Improvement Quarterly* 28(4): 71-89.

Huselid, M.A., and B.E. Becker. 2000. Comment on "Measurement Error in Research on Human Resources and Firm Performance: How Much Error Is There and How Does It Influence Effect Size Estimates?" by Gerhart, Wright, McMahan, and Snell. *Personnel Psychology* 53(4): 835-854.

Impact International. 2011. *Aligning Training With Corporate Strategy*. Whitepaper. www.impactinternational.com/aligning-training-corporate-strategy.

Jin, Y., M.M. Hopkins, and J.L.S. Wittmer. 2010. "Linking Human Capital to Competitive Advantages: Flexibility in a Manufacturing Firm's Supply Chain." *Human Resource Management* 49(5): 939-963.

Kaplan, R.S., and D.P. Norton. 2004. "Measuring the Strategic Readiness of Intangible Assets." *Harvard Business Review* 82(2): 52-63.

Kaufman, R. 1998. *Strategic Planning Plus: An Organizational Guide (Revised)*. Newbury Park, CA: Sage Publishing.

Kaufman, R. 2004. "Seven Deadly Sins of Strategic Planning." ASTD Links. American Society for Training & Development, Alexandria, VA.

Kaufman, R. 2011. *The Manager's Pocket Guide to Mega Thinking and Planning*. Amherst, MA: HRD Press.

Kaufman, R.A. 2000. *Mega Planning: Practical Tools for Organizational Success*. Thousand Oaks, CA: Sage Publications.

Kaufman, R.A. 2006. *Change, Choices, and Consequences: A Guide to Mega Thinking and Planning*. Amherst, MA: HRD Press.

Kaufman, R., and R. Clark. 1999. "Re-Establishing Performance Improvement as A Legitimate Area of Inquiry, Activity, And Contribution: Rules of the Road." *Performance Improvement* 38(9): 13-18.

Kaufman, R., and I. Guerra. 2002. "A Perspective Adjustment to Add Value to External Clients, Including Society." *Human Resource Development Quarterly* 13(1): 109-115.

Kaufman, R., and I. Guerra-López. 2013. Alexandria, VA: ASTD Press.

Kaufman, R., R. Watkins, M. Stith, D. Triner. 1998. "The Changing Corporate Mind: Organizations, Vision, Missions, Purposes, and Indicators on the Move Toward Societal Payoffs." *Performance Improvement Quarterly* 11(3): 32-44.

Kluger, A.N., and A. DeNisi. 1996. "The Effects of Feedback Interventions on Performance: A Historical Review, a Meta-Analysis, and a Preliminary Feedback Intervention Theory." *Psychological Bulletin* 119: 254-284.

Kotter, J. 1996. "Leading Change: Why Transformation Efforts Fail." *Harvard Business Review* 73(2): 59–67.

Kraiger, K., D. McLinden, and W.J. Casper. 2004. "Collaborative Planning for Training Impact." *Human Resource Management* 43(4): 337-351. DOI: 10.1002/hrm.20028.

Lewin, K. 1951. *Field Theory in Social Science.* New York: Harper and Row.

Luftman, J. 2003. "Assessing IT/Business Alignment." *Information Systems Management* 20(4): 9-15.

Lynch, R.L., and K.F. Cross. 1991. *Measure Up! How to Measure Corporate Performance.* Cambridge, MA: Blackwell.

Maskell, B. 1992. *Performance Measurement for World Class Manufacturing: A Model for American Companies.* New York: Productivity Press.

Montesino, M.U. 2002. "Strategic Alignment of Training, Transfer-Enhancing Behaviors, and Training Usage: A Posttraining Study." *Human Resource Development Quarterly* 13(1): 89-108.

Nankervis, A.R., and R.L. Compton. 2006. "Performance Management: Theory in Practice?" *Asia Pacific Journal of Human Resources* 44: 83-101. doi:10.1177/1038411106061509.

Nathan, R.P. 2009. "Point/Counterpoint." *Journal of Policy Analysis and Management* 28: 496-516. doi:10.1002/pam.20232.

Neely, A., C. Adams, M. Kennerley. 2002. *The Performance Prism: The Scorecard for Measuring and Managing Business Success.* London: FT Prentice-Hall.

Niven, P.R. 2006. *Balanced Scorecard Step by Step: Maximizing Performance and Maintaining Results.* Hoboken, NJ: John Wiley & Sons.

Nutt, P. 2007. "Intelligence Gathering for Decision Making." *Omega* 35: 604-622.

Nutt, P.C. 2008. "Investigating the Success of Decision Making Processes." *Journal of Management Studies* 45: 425-455. doi:10.1111/j.1467-6486.2007.00756.x.

Oracle. 2011. "Customer Experience Impact Report: Getting to the heart of Consumer and Brand Relationship." www.oracle.com/us/products/applications/cust-exp-impact-report-epss-1560493.pdf.

Paauwe, J. 2009. "HRM Performance: Achievements, Methodological Issues and Prospects." *Journal of Management Studies* 46(1): 129-142. http://dx.doi.org/10.1111/j.1467-6486.2008.00809.x.

Porter, M. 1996. "What Is Strategy?" *Harvard Business Review.* November-December, 4-21.

Pound, J. 1995. "The Promise of the Governed Corporation." *Harvard Business Review.* March-April.

Pulakos, E.D., and R.S. O'Leary. 2011. "Why Is Performance Management Broken?" *Industrial and Organizational Psychology* 4: 146-164. doi: 10.1111/j.1754-9434.2011.01315.x.

Rummler, G.A., and A.P. Brache. 1995. *Improving Performance: How to Manage the White Space on the Organization Chart.* Jossey-Bass: San Francisco.

Singh, S., T.K. Darwish, A.C. Costa, and N. Anderson. 2012. "Measuring HRM and Organisational Performance: Concepts, Issues, and Framework." *Management Decision* 50(4): 651-667.

Sleezer, K., J. Hough, and D. Gradous. 1998 "Measurement Challenges in Evaluation and Performance Improvement." *Performance Improvement Quarterly* 11(4): 62-75.

Smith, M. 2002. "Implementing Organizational Change: Correlates of Success and Failure." *Performance Improvement Quarterly* 15(1): 67-83.

Ulrich, D., and W. Brockbank. 2009. "The HR Business-Partner Model: Past Learning and Future Challenges." *Human Resource Planning* 32(2): 5-7.

Van Iddekinge, C.H., G.R. Ferris, P.L. Perrewe, F.R. Blass, T.D. Heetderks, and A.A. Perryman. 2009. "Effects of Selection and Training on Unit-Level Performance Over Time: A Latent Growth Modeling Approach." *Journal of Applied Psychology* 94(4): 829.

Wells, D.L., R.H. Moorman, and J.M. Werner. 2007. "The Impact of the Perceived Purpose of Electronic Performance Monitoring on an Array of Attitudinal Variables." *Human Resource Development Quarterly* 18(1): 121-138.

Wright, P.C., and M. Belcourt. 1995. "Costing Training Activity: A Decision Maker's Dilemma." *Management Decision* 33(2): 5-15.

About the Authors

Ingrid Guerra-López, PhD, is an internationally recognized performance improvement expert and bestselling author. She is the chief executive officer of the Institute for Needs Assessment and Evaluation, a firm that provides consulting, coaching, and training and development services focused on strategic measurement, management, and alignment of learning and performance improvement programs. Ingrid is also a professor at Wayne State University, where she conducts research and teaches graduate courses focused on performance measurement, management, and strategic alignment. She recently completed a term as director on the board of the International Society for Performance Improvement, and completed her tenure as editor-in-chief of Performance Improvement Quarterly.

Ingrid has authored seven books, including Needs Assessment for Organizational Success and Performance Evaluation: Proven Approaches to Improving Programs and Organizations. She has also authored approximately 100 articles and facilitated hundreds of international and national presentations and workshops on topics related to performance assessment, monitoring and evaluation, and strategic alignment. Her clients include international development agencies, government, education, military, healthcare, and corporate organizations. Ingrid has coached and mentored hundreds of graduate students, executives, managers, and other professionals, disseminating evidenced-based performance improvement practices internationally in more than 30 countries.

Karen Hicks, PhD, has more than 15 years' experience in training and development strategy and implementation. She has led and managed the transition of learning functions from traditional to transformational strategic contributors. In her research and practice, Karen works with organizations to build measurement and evaluation capabilities and to demonstrate the strategic value of their work through strategic alignment assessment and continuous improvement. Karen has published academic and practitioner articles in *Performance Improvement, Journal of Business and Technology, Performance Improvement Quarterly, Evaluation and Program Planning*. She has also written a *TD at Work* issue, and presents her work at ISPI, ATD, SHRM, and AAHLE national and local conferences..

Index